10 Minute Guide to Freelance Graphics® for Windows™ 2

Jenna Christen

A Division of Macmillan Computer Publishing
201 W. 103rd St., Indianapolis, Indiana 46290 USA

*To Jerry, for the fun times, the friendship, and—of course
—the volleyball.*

© 1993 by Que® Corporation

International Standard Book Number: 1-56761-182-6
Library of Congress Catalog Card Number: 93-70251

96 95   7 6 5

Interpretation of the printing code: the rightmost double-digit number is the year of the book's printing; the rightmost single-digit number is the number of the book's printing. For example, a printing code of 93-1 shows that the first printing of the book was in 1993.

Publisher: *Marie Butler-Knight*
Associate Publisher: *Lisa A. Bucki*
Managing Editor: *Elizabeth Keaffaber*
Acquisitions Manager: *Stephen R. Poland*
Development Editor: *Kelly Oliver*
Production Editor: *Annalise N. Di Paolo*
Copy Editor: *San Dee Phillips*
Cover Designer: *Dan Armstrong*
Designer: *Amy Peppler-Adams*
Indexer: *C. Alan Small*
Production: *Diana Bigham, Katy Bodenmiller, Tim Cox, Mark Enochs, Linda Koopman, Tom Loveman, Beth Rago, Joe Ramon, Carrie Roth, Greg Simsic*

Special thanks to C. Herbert Feltner for ensuring the technical accuracy of this book.

Screen reproductions in this book were created by means of the program Collage Plus from Inner Media, Inc., Hollis, NH.

Printed in the United States of America

Contents

12 Creating a Line Chart, 69

13 Creating a High-Low-Close-Open Chart, 75

14 Creating an Organization Chart, 80

15 Creating a Table, 86

16 Editing a Table, 90

17 Printing Your Presentation, 98

18 Adding Symbols to Your Presentation, 103

Introduction

If you have never used a presentation graphics program before, you will be delighted by the features Freelance Graphics for Windows offers. You'll be amazed at how fast and easily you can generate top-quality presentation matcrials. Remember how you labored to produce professional-looking overhead masters, slides, and audience handouts with your word processor or desktop publisher? Well, what may have taken days before will now take only a few hours.

Freelance Graphics' QuickStart program, an on-line tutorial, walks you through several important steps of the presentation process. The Freelance Graphics Autographix Slide Service allows you to send your presentation files via modem directly to a print house where they can be processed into 35mm slides. If your computer system has multimedia capabilities, you can add sound and video to your presentations using the Lotus Media Manager. Finally, the valuable SmartMaster sets design your presentations for you (such as font, color, and graphics) so you can concentrate on the content of your presentation.

How to Use This Book

The *10 Minute Guide* series is a unique approach to learning computer programs. Each lesson is designed to be completed in 10 minutes or less and includes steps that teach you how to perform a specific task. Many of the screen configurations that will appear on your computer monitor as you perform the steps are illustrated in this book to show you what to expect.

If you are new to Windows, you should review the Microsoft Windows Primer at the end of this book before attempting to work through this guide. If you need help installing Freelance Graphics on your system, turn to the inside front cover of this book for instructions.

Once you are familiar with Windows and have installed Freelance Graphics, you can complete the lessons in this book either consecutively or by skipping from lesson to lesson. It isn't necessary to work through the lessons in order.

Conventions Used in This Book

The following icons point out definitions, cautions, and tips to help you as you work through each lesson in this book:

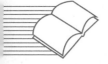

Plain English icons tell you that a term is being defined.

Panic Button icons appear when remedies are offered to troublesome situations.

Timesaver Tips point out ways for you to use the program more effectively.

Additionally, the following conventions are used to aid you as you work through the lessons:

Menu items or dialog box options	Each menu item and dialog box option you are told to select will appear in color.
On-screen text	Text that appears on-screen is formatted in a special computer font.
Menu, dialog box, and window names	The first letter of each menu, dialog box, or window name is capitalized.
What you type	The information you type is printed in bold computer type and color.
Selection letters	The selection letter of each command or option is bold.
Key combinations	In many cases, you must press a two-key combination in order to enter a command. For example, "Press Alt+X." In such cases, hold down the first key, and press the second key.

Acknowledgments

It was a pleasure working with the team at Que Corporation. Special thanks to Marie Butler-Knight, publisher, and to Steve Poland for his patience during the early stages of the writing process. A big "thank you" to Kelly Oliver—one of the most considerate and supportive editors I've encountered. Lastly, credit should go to Annalise Di Paolo and San Dee Phillips for ensuring the production quality of this book.

Trademarks

An Introduction to Freelance Graphics for Windows

In this lesson, you will learn how Freelance Graphics for Windows creates your presentations and how to use the Help feature.

What Is a Presentation?

Presentations prove a point, propose an action, relay information, or present an idea. They are usually delivered in the form of a slide show, using 35mm slides or overhead transparencies. However, you can use Freelance Graphics to produce more than just slides or overhead masters. You can create

Handouts to accompany your presentation. These hand-outs can include two, four, or six slides on each printed page.

Audience notes if the audience is expected to take notes during the presentation. Freelance Graphics prints one slide on the top half of the printed page and blank lines on the bottom half of the page for notes.

Speaker notes to record information about each page in a presentation. A speaker note is a note you create and

1

attach to a presentation that is not part of the actual presentation. Freelance Graphics lets you create one speaker note for each page in your presentation.

A Screen show instead of slides or overheads. Freelance Graphics displays your presentation page by page on a computer screen. You can use the mouse to move to the next screen, or you can automate the screen show so that it moves from slide to slide automatically.

Starting Freelance Graphics for Windows

You should have a basic understanding of Microsoft Windows before you start Freelance Graphics for Windows. If you need a refresher course on the Windows environment, review the Microsoft Windows Primer at the end of this book.

Haven't Installed Yet? If you haven't installed Freelance Graphics for Windows and need help, turn to the inside front cover for instructions on installing Freelance Graphics on your system.

The first time you start Freelance Graphics, the program invites you to watch a quick tutorial. After the first time, you won't be asked to view the tutorial; the program will start with the standard Welcome to Freelance Graphics window. To start Freelance Graphics for the first time, perform the following steps:

1. Start Windows, and display the Program Manager window.

2. The Freelance Graphics program icon is located in the Lotus Applications group. If this group is not currently showing, open the Window menu, and select Lotus Applications.

3. Select the Freelance Graphics program icon.

4. If you have started Freelance Graphics before, you'll see the Welcome to Freelance Graphics dialog box (Figure 1.2). Otherwise, a dialog box will appear inviting you to watch a brief animated tutorial of Freelance Graphics (Figure 1.1). Choose OK.

5. Freelance Graphics' Quick Tour will explain, in simple terms, how the program works. When it's over, you can select options from the screen in Figure 1.1.

Select Quit to exit QuickStart.

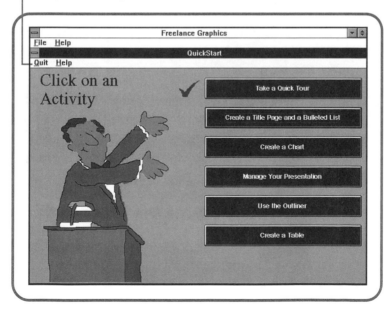

Figure 1.1 The QuickStart Screen.

6. In order to skip the rest of the tutorial and begin the program at the standard Welcome to Freelance Graphics window, select **Q**uit on the menu bar.

7. A dialog box will appear asking you to confirm your decision to quit. Select **Q**uit Quick Start. The screen in Figure 1.2 will appear.

At this point, you will be able to choose between **C**reate a new presentation and **W**ork on an existing presentation (see Lesson 2).

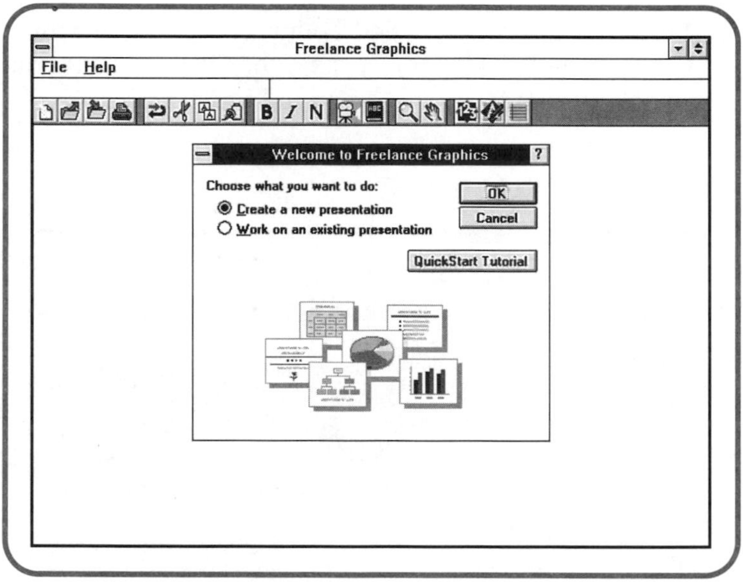

Figure 1.2 The Welcome to Freelance Graphics dialog box.

A Look at the Application Window

The Freelance Graphics window contains the typical Windows elements: title, menu and scroll bars, an icon palette, Minimize and Restore buttons, and so on. The descriptions in Table 1.1 will familiarize you with the rest of the Freelance Graphics window elements that you will use as you create your presentation.

Table 1.1 Freelance Graphics Window Elements.

Icon	Name/Description
Page 1 of 1	**Page Locator icon** Displays current page number. Click the left arrow to move to the previous page. Click the right arrow to move to the next page.
Page Layout...	**Page Layout icon** Click on this icon to assign a different page layout for the new page.
New Page...	**New Page icon** Click on this icon to assign a different page layout for the current page.
◼◻	**Color/Black & White icon** Use this icon to display your presentation in color or in black and white.
⬜	**Display/Hide icon** Use this icon to display or hide the SmartIcon palette.
Arial MT	**Font icon** Use this icon to change the font of the selected text.
27.1	**Point Size icon** Use this icon to change the point size of the selected text.
▤	**Outliner icon** Click on this icon to change to the Outliner view.

continues

Table 1.1   Continued.

Icon	Name/Description
	**Page Sorter icon** Click on this icon to change to the Page Sorter view.
	Current Page icon Click on this icon to switch the page currently selected in the Page Sorter or the Outliner to full size.

Using the Help Feature

Freelance Graphics provides an extensive on-line Help feature to help you perform virtually any task. To get help at any time, pull down the Help menu, and select Contents, or press F1. A Help window opens, displaying a list of Help topics. Scroll through the list, and select the topic of your choice. A second window opens containing helpful instructions or definitions for the topic you chose.

Context-Sensitive Help   Nearly every Freelance Graphics dialog box has a question mark icon located in the upper-right corner of the box (see Figure 1.2 for an example). Click on this button to display helpful information about the dialog box functions.

Using the Help Window Buttons

The buttons in Table 1.2 are located at the top of the **Help** window. They allow you to move through the help system with ease.

Table 1.2   The buttons on the Help menu.

Button	Function
Contents	Displays a list of **Help** topics.
Search	Displays a detailed index of **Help** items. Finds a topic for you after you type the topic's name or part of its name.
Back	Brings you back to the previous **Help** window.
History	Shows a list of all the **Help** topics opened thus far.
<<	Moves you to the previous **Help** screen in the series.
>>	Advances you to the next **Help** screen in the series.

In this lesson, you learned how Freelance Graphics for Windows creates your presentations and how to use the **Help** feature. In the next lesson, you will discover how to create or open a presentation.

Lesson 2

Creating and Opening a Presentation

In this lesson, you will learn how to create and open a presentation.

Creating a Presentation

In the quick tutorial that you watched the first time you started Freelance Graphics, three basic steps to creating a presentation were emphasized:

- Choosing a look

- Choosing a page layout

- Filling in the blanks

This lesson will explain some of the details involved in these three steps.

Choosing a Look

Freelance Graphics comes with 65 SmartMaster sets. To help you decide which SmartMaster set is the most appropriate for the presentation you plan to create, you can view each set in the Choose a Look for Your Presentation dialog box. You can also review them in the *SmartMaster Sets and Symbols* booklet that accompanies Freelance Graphics.

What Is a SmartMaster Set?   A SmartMaster set is a collection of predesigned page layouts that serve as templates for a presentation. Each SmartMaster set contains eleven page layouts which provide fill-in-the-blank formats. The SmartMaster set you use determines the overall design of your presentation.

Choosing the Page Layout

When you have selected the design for your presentation, Freelance Graphics asks you to specify the page on which you want to work. You can start from the beginning and work on the title page, or you can jump to the next page and develop a bulleted list.

What Is a Page Layout?   The eleven types of page layouts range from charts and tables to bulleted lists. Each page layout is designed for a specific part of your presentation; for instance, the Title page layout is normally used for the first page of your presentation, and the 2 Charts page layout is an ideal layout to use when comparing two different charts.

Starting a Presentation

When you start Freelance Graphics, the Welcome to Freelance Graphics dialog box appears. If you want to work on a new presentation, follow these steps:

1. Choose Create a new presentation, and select OK.

Already Working? After you've started to work, you can begin a new presentation at any time. To start a new presentation, open the File menu and select New, or select the New File icon.

2. The Choose a Look for Your Presentation dialog box appears (see Figure 2.1).

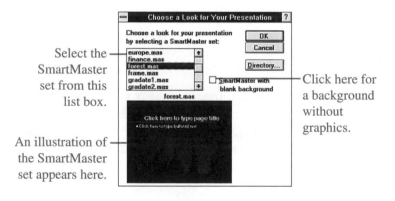

Figure 2.1 The Choose a Look for Your Presentation dialog box.

3. In the box containing the SmartMaster set names, select the SmartMaster set you want. An illustration of that SmartMaster set appears in the sample box.

4. If you want a blank background (one with no graphics) for your presentation, select the SmartMaster with blank background check box.

5. Select OK. Freelance Graphics displays the Choose Page Layout dialog box shown in Figure 2.2.

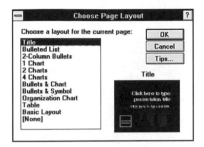

Figure 2.2   Select the page you want in the Choose Page Layout dialog box.

6. To see what each page layout looks like in the particular design (the SmartMaster set) you've specified, select each page layout and review the corresponding illustration in the sample box.

7. When you've chosen the page layout on which you want to work, select that page layout.

The Freelance Graphics application window appears when you select OK. The first page of your presentation, formatted with the page layout and SmartMaster design you selected, rests inside the application window (see Figure 2.3).

New file icon

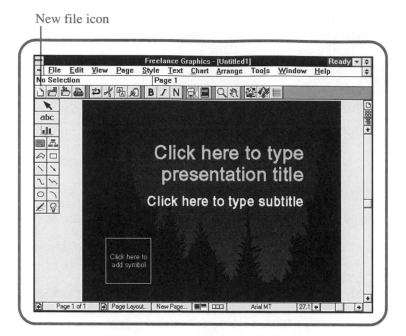

Figure 2.3 The Freelance Graphics application window.

Opening an Existing Presentation

To retrieve a file while working in Freelance Graphics, choose the File menu, and select Open, or select the File Open icon. The Open File dialog box appears (see Figure 2.4). Follow these steps to open a file:

1. In the File Name text box, select the name of the presentation you want to open. Use the Directories and Drives boxes if you need to retrieve the file from another location.

2. If you want to close the presentation in the active window first and bring the new file into the same window, mark the **R**eplace current file check box.

3. To keep the current presentation open after you retrieve the new presentation, make sure the **R**eplace current file check box is not marked. You can work on up to nine presentations at once (depending on how much available memory your system has).

4. Select OK. Freelance Graphics opens the presentation you selected.

Select the presentation you want to open.

	Open File	?
File **n**ame:	**D**irectories:	OK
.pre	c:\flw\work	Cancel
boardmtg.pre	c:\	
littonpr.pre	flw	☐ **R**eplace
proposal.pre	work	current file
	Drives:	
	c: ares	
File **t**ypes:		
Presentation (PRE)		
File information:		

Click here to close the current window
before the new one is opened.

Figure 2.4 Choose the presentation you want to open.

Fast Retrievals At the end of the **F**ile menu, Freelance Graphics displays the names of up to the last five files opened. If you want to retrieve one of these files, open the **F**ile menu, and then select the appropriate file name.

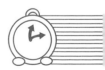

You can choose **W**ork on an existing presentation from the Welcome to Freelance Graphics dialog box to open a file you have already saved. When you choose this option, Freelance Graphics displays the Choose Presentation dialog box instead of the File Open dialog box, but they work the same way.

In this lesson, you learned how to create and open a new or existing presentation. In the next lesson, you will learn how to save and close your presentations, and how to exit Freelance Graphics.

Lesson 3

Saving and Closing Presentations

In this lesson, you will learn how to save and close presentations and how to exit Freelance Graphics.

Saving a Presentation

It's a good idea to name and save a presentation immediately after you open it. From that point on, you select the File Save icon to save any changes, which you should do periodically to prevent losses. If you don't save a file right after you open it, you may not remember to save it until a large amount of data has been entered. This is dangerous because that data is susceptible to being lost the entire time the presentation remains unsaved.

To save a presentation for the first time, perform the following steps:

1. Open the File menu, and select Save, select the File Save icon, or press Ctrl+S. The Save As dialog box appears, as shown in Figure 3.1.

File Save icon

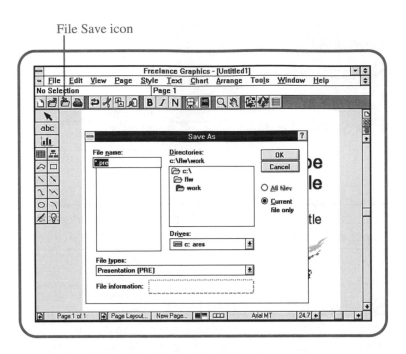

Figure 3.1   The Save As dialog box.

2. In the File **n**ame text box, type a file name (up to eight characters). You don't need to assign a file name extension; Freelance Graphics automatically adds the extension .PRE.

3. If you wish to save the file to a different disk drive, pull down the Dri**v**es drop-down list and choose the appropriate drive letter.

4. To save the file to a different directory, select the desired directory in the **D**irectories box.

5. Select OK. The file is saved to disk and remains open in the application window.

If you save new changes to a file that has already been saved, Freelance Graphics asks you whether you want to replace or back up the file. Make your selection, keeping the following in mind:

> If you choose **R**eplace, Freelance Graphics replaces the old version of the file with a new one, incorporating the changes you made since you last saved the original file.

> If you choose **B**ackup, Freelance Graphics leaves the original file intact but moves it to a different directory (the backup directory specified in User Setup dialog box). The new version of the file is saved under the original name and directory.

Later, Message   If you don't want Freelance Graphics to question whether or not you want to back up a file each time you save it, you can disable the File Replace message using the Tools User Setup menu command.

Automatic Saves   Freelance Graphics can automatically save your files at set intervals as you work on your presentation. Open the Tools menu, and select User Setup. In the User Setup dialog box, mark the Auto timed save check box, and specify the time between file saves.

To save a file under a different name, or to save the file to a different directory or disk drive, open the File menu, and select the Save As command. Enter a new name in the Save As dialog box, or choose a different directory or drive.

Closing a Presentation

It is not necessary to close a presentation in order to work on another one. If two presentations are open, you will only see the newer one. To switch back to the first presentation, open the Window menu and select the name of that presentation. If you're sure you won't work on a presentation again, you should close it. To close a presentation, perform the following steps:

1. Make sure the window you want to close is active (meaning, the insertion point rests inside it).

2. Open the File menu, and select Close. If you haven't saved the file or the most recent changes, Freelance Graphics asks you whether you want to save the changes.

3. To close the file without saving any changes, select No. The window closes.

4. To save your changes, select OK. If you have previously saved the file, the changes are saved and the window closes. If this is an unsaved presentation, the Save As dialog box appears. Complete this dialog box following the instructions in the "Saving a Presentation" section earlier in this lesson.

Exiting Freelance Graphics

To quit Freelance Graphics, perform any of the following steps:

- Select the Control menu box located in the upper left corner of the Freelance Graphics application window.

- Press Alt+F4.

- Open the File menu, and select Exit.

    An Exit Freelance Graphics icon is available for you to place on the icon palette permanently, if you want. Use the Tools SmartIcons command to do so.

    In this lesson, you learned how to save and close your presentation and how to exit Freelance Graphics. In the next lesson, you will learn how to add new pages to your presentation.

Lesson 4

Adding New Pages to Your Presentation

In this lesson, you will learn how to add new pages to your presentation.

Adding a New Page

Adding a new page is an important step in the development of your presentation. You need to think about which page layout will best convey the information you wish to present to your audience. When it is time for you to create a new page, you must choose a page layout from the eleven available layouts (see Figure 4.1 for a complete list of these layouts).

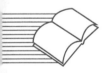

What Is a Page Layout? A page layout is basically a fill-in-the-blanks template. Later lessons describe the eleven available layouts that provide every type of page you'll need for your presentation, including bulleted lists, charts, tables, and more.

After you have decided on the type of page layout you want to use, follow these steps to add a new page to your presentation:

1. Open the **P**age menu, and select New; or select the New Page box at the bottom of the application window. The New Page dialog box appears, as shown in Figure 4.1.

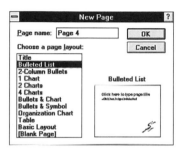

Figure 4.1   The New Page dialog box.

2. In the **P**age name box, type a name for the page.

3. Select the type of page layout you want. In the lower right corner of the dialog box, Freelance Graphics illustrates what the page will look like. Select each page layout if you want to see how each page looks under the current SmartMaster set.

4. Select OK. The new page opens, and you are now ready to type text or add graphics objects (see Figure 4.2).

Instant New Page   If you want to create a new page using the same format of the page currently displayed, you can bypass the preceding steps and simply press F7.

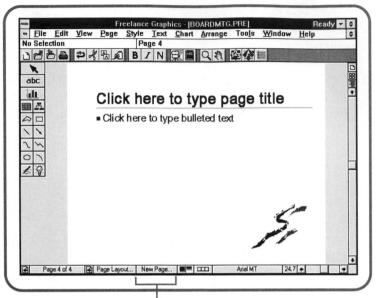

Click the New Page box to add a new page.

Figure 4.2   Freelance Graphics creates the page you specified.

Moving from Page to Page   Select the left arrow icon at the bottom of the application window to move to the previous page and on the right arrow icon to move to the next page.

In this lesson, you learned how to insert new pages into your presentation. In the next lesson, you will learn how to enter and edit text.

Lesson 5

Entering and Editing Text

In this lesson, you will learn how to use text blocks to insert text into a presentation and how to edit that text.

Entering Text

Adding text to a Freelance Graphics presentation is not like entering text using a word processor or desktop publisher. Any text you add to the presentation must be inserted into a *text block*.

Text Blocks   Freelance Graphics text blocks do more than just hold text. Since they are objects as well, text blocks can be repositioned on a presentation page, resized, copied, and deleted like any other object.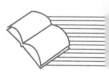

There are regular text blocks and Click here . . . text blocks. Each page layout has predesigned Click here . . . text blocks for your use (see Figure 5.1 for an example). If the supplied blocks do not meet your needs, you can create regular text blocks to insert additional text.

Text icon   Click here . . . text blocks

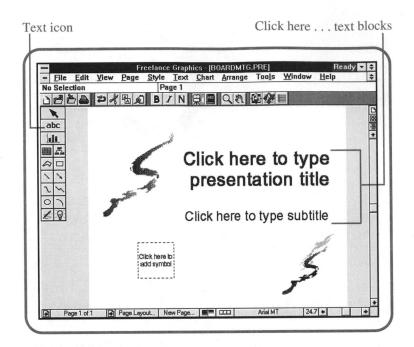

Figure 5.1   A Title page layout with Click here . . . text blocks.

Using Click here . . . Text Blocks

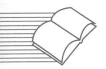

What Is a Click here . . . Text Block?   Each page layout provides Click here . . . text blocks, which are rectangles into which you can type new text. The text assumes the attributes specified in the text block, including font, size, color, and alignment. The prompt text (Click here . . .) does not print or appear in screen shows. Only text you enter will print or be displayed in a screen show.

To enter text on a presentation page, perform the following steps:

1. Click on Click here . . . text block. Freelance Graphics displays a box you use to enter text, as shown in Figure 5.2.

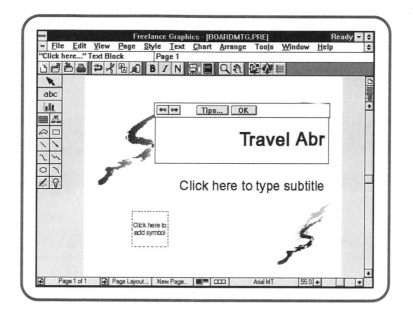

Figure 5.2   Using a Click here . . . text block.

Help!   If you need help in a text box, select the Tips button.

2. Type the text you want. Freelance Graphics wraps the text automatically when the text reaches the right margin of the block.

3. If you need to start a new paragraph, press Enter.

4. Select OK. The box closes and the text you entered replaces the Click here . . . prompt (see Figure 5.3).

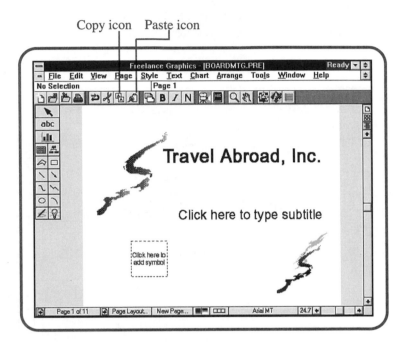

Figure 5.3 The new text replaces the Click here . . . prompt.

Creating New Text Blocks

You can add regular text blocks to a presentation page where there is no available Click here . . . text blocks, or where additional text blocks are needed. For example, you may wish to add a comment beside a chart. To create a text block, perform the following steps:

1. Click on the Text icon (the abc icon) in the Toolbox, located at the left side of the screen.

2. Move the mouse pointer to the place on the presentation page where you want the text to begin.

3. If you want to confine the text to a certain area (so that it wraps automatically), hold down the left mouse button and drag the mouse to draw a rectangle. A dotted line will appear to show you the size of the rectangle. When you've reached the correct size, let go of the mouse button. A box appears into which you can type new text.

Be Careful Creating That Rectangle If you draw a rectangle over an existing text block, Freelance Graphics thinks you want to select and edit the existing text block rather than create a new one.

4. If you don't want the text to wrap automatically, don't draw a rectangle. Just select where you want the text to begin.

5. Type the new text in the box.

6. Select OK. The box closes, and the new text appears on the presentation page.

If you need to add new text, or modify or delete text you've entered, follow the instructions in the next section. If you want to change the look of the text, see Lesson 6, "Changing Text Attributes."

27

Editing Text

You can alter the text inside a text block, or you can move or change the size of the block itself. Follow the steps below to modify text inside of a text block. However, if you wish to change the location of a text block or alter its dimensions, review Lesson 20, "Managing Objects."

To add new text or to select, copy, move, or delete existing text inside of a text block, perform the following steps:

1. Select the text block you want to edit. The text block is now selected.

2. Open the Text menu, and select Edit; or press F2, or select the text block again. The box which appeared earlier when you first entered the text appears again with the insertion point resting inside. This means Text Edit Mode is now in effect; you are ready to enter new text or edit existing text.

   To add new text Place the insertion point where you want the new text to begin, and type the text.

   To select text Place the insertion point in front of the text to be selected. Hold down the left mouse button and drag the mouse pointer over all of the desired text. Once you've finished selecting the text, let go of the mouse button. The text is now highlighted.

   To copy text First select it. Then open the Edit menu, and select Copy, or select the Copy icon. Next, place the insertion point where you want to insert the copied text. (To copy text to a different text block, select that block first.) Open the Edit menu, and select Paste; or select the Paste icon.

To move text   First select it and then follow the instructions for copying text, with this exception: after opening the Edit menu the first time, select Cut.

To delete text   First select it. Then press Delete, or open the Edit menu, and select Clear. The text disappears.

Editing a Series of Text Blocks   You can quickly edit multiple text blocks on one page or in a group of presentation pages. After you have finished editing the first text block (following the steps in the next section), place the insertion point at the top line of the text block. Then use the up and down arrows to move to other text blocks on the same page, or Page Down and Page Up to move to text blocks on other presentation pages.

Curving Text

You can curve a line of text into different shapes: circles, boxes, arcs, S curves, bell curves, diagonal lines, peaks, triangles, and so on. Some shapes may not be available, however, depending on how many characters you are trying to curve.

The Curve Text Command Is Dimmed   You cannot curve text that was entered into a Click here . . . text block without first moving that text out of the text block. To do so, hold down the Ctrl key and drag the text out of the block. Notice that the original Click here . . . prompt reappears. The text you dragged appears in a new, regular text block and can now be curved.

To curve text, perform the following steps:

1. Select the text block containing the text you want to curve.

2. Open the Text menu, and select Curved Text. The Curved Text dialog box appears, as shown in Figure 5.4.

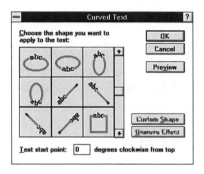

Figure 5.4   Pick a curve in this dialog box.

3. Use the scroll box to display different shapes. Select the shape you want.

4. For circular text (such as circles and ovals), enter a starting point next to Text start point. This specifies the angle at which the curve will start (based on 360 degrees). For example, entering 180 will cause the curve to start at 6 o'clock.

5. To see what the text will look like, hold down the left mouse button on the Preview button until the sample appears. Release the mouse button when you are done previewing the sample.

6. Select OK. Freelance Graphics curves the text as specified.

Adding a Text Block Border and Pattern

You can spruce up the look of your presentation text by adding borders around a text block or by filling the text block with a color or pattern. To create a border or fill a text block, perform these steps:

1. Select the text block you want to change.

2. Open the Text menu, and select Frame. The Text Frame dialog box appears (see Figure 5.5).

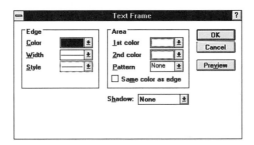

Figure 5.5 The Text Frame dialog box.

3. To add a border, specify a Color, Width, and Style in the Edge box. If you desire a shadow effect for the border, make sure you specify a line style, and then specify a shadow in the Shadow box.

4. To fill the text block with color, specify one or two colors in the Area section.

5. If you want to include a background pattern, choose a pattern in the **P**attern box in the Area section.

6. Click on OK. Freelance Graphics applies the specifications you made to the selected text block.

In this lesson, you learned how to enter and edit text. In the next lesson, you will learn how to change the look of text.

Lesson 6
Changing Text Attributes

In this lesson, you will learn how to change the attributes of selected text and paragraph styles.

To change the attributes of a particular letter, word, or group of words in a text block, you should select the text you want to change and apply new settings to this text only, leaving the rest of the text in the text block intact. On the other hand, if you wish to change various attributes of an entire paragraph in the text block, you should use the Paragraph Styles dialog box and change the paragraph style itself.

Paragraph Styles Each text block has three predesigned paragraph styles. Each style determines the attributes of all text at that style level. Paragraph styles control font, point size, color, alignment, bullets, spacing, indents, and attributes, such as boldface, italics, and underlining.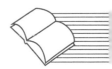

Formatting Selected Text

To select specific text and override the paragraph style attributes assigned to it, perform the following steps:

1. Click on the text block containing the text you want to change.

2. Open the Text menu, and select Edit; press F2, or click on the text block again to enter the text edit mode.

3. Highlight the text you want to change by dragging the mouse over it.

4. Use SmartIcons items on the Text menu, or accelerator keys, to change as many attributes as you want. For example, to make text boldface, click on the Bold icon, press Ctrl+B, or open the Text menu, and select Bold. Or to italicize the text, click on the Italics icon, press Ctrl+I, or open the Text menu, and select Italic.

Removing Special Emphasis   To remove all attributes from selected text, open the Text menu, and select Normal, or click on the Normal Text icon.

After you have made all desired changes, click anywhere outside of the text block. The edit box closes and the text appears in the new format.

How Do I Revert to the Original Style?   If you don't like the results of the formatting changes you've made to selected text, you can quickly return the text to its original state, rather than undoing every attribute you changed. With the text still highlighted, simply open the Text menu, and select Reset To Style.

Modifying Paragraph Styles

Each text block has three paragraph styles assigned to it, called level 1, level 2, and level 3 styles. If you want to alter the look of a paragraph in a text block, you can assign a different style level to the paragraph and see if that works. If not, you can modify the paragraph style settings in the Paragraph Styles dialog box to format the paragraph exactly as you'd like it.

Switching Style Levels

To assign a different paragraph style level to a paragraph in a text block, follow these steps:

1. Click on the text block containing the paragraph you want to modify.

2. Open the Text menu, and select Edit; press F2, or click on the text block again to enter the text edit mode. The edit box appears, as shown in Figure 6.1.

3. Click anywhere on the paragraph you want to change.

4. Click on the Demote icon (the right arrow), or press Tab to move from level 1 to level 2 or from level 2 to level 3. The look of the paragraph changes after you switch levels. Notice how the paragraphs in Figure 6.2 have changed from their appearance in Figure 6.1 now that style 2 has been assigned to them.

Promote icon   Demote icon

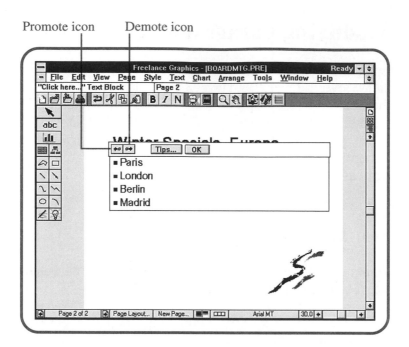

Figure 6.1   Use the Promote and Demote icons to switch style levels.

5. Click on the Promote icon (left arrow), or press Shift+Tab to move from style 3 to style 2 or from style 2 to style 1.

6. When you have finished changing styles, click anywhere outside of the text block. The edit box disappears, and the text appears in the new format.

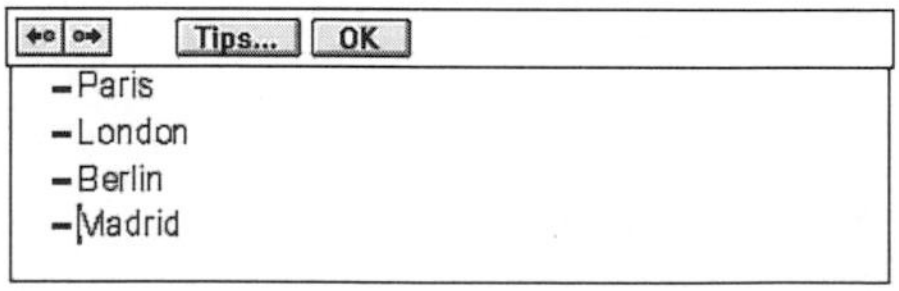

Figure 6.2   The paragraph looks different at level 2.

Changing Paragraph Style Settings

When you make changes to a paragraph style (in the Paragraph Styles dialog box), the changes are reflected in all paragraphs using that style level in the text block. To change the attributes for one or more paragraph style levels, follow these procedures:

1. Double-click on the text block whose styles you want to modify. Alternatively, you can click on the text block, open the Style menu, and select Attributes. The Paragraph Styles dialog box appears, as shown in Figure 6.3.

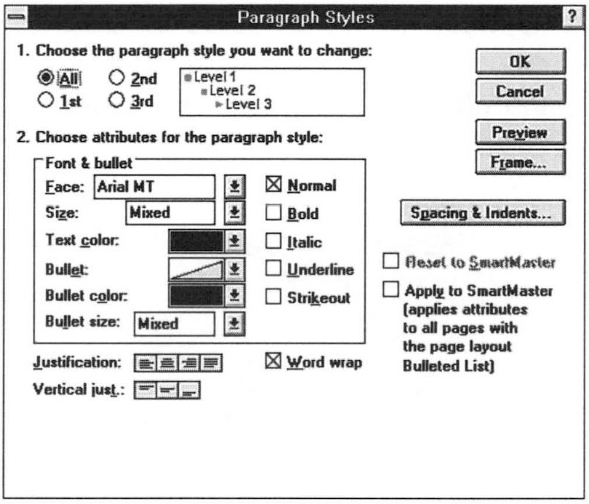

Figure 6.3 The Paragraph Styles dialog box.

2. Choose the style you want to modify. If you select All, the attributes you specify will apply to all three styles.

3. Select the attributes you want in the Font & bullet box. To use numbered bullets, select 1 in the Bullet drop-down list.

4. Change the horizontal justification to make text left-aligned, right-aligned, centered, or justified. Change the vertical justification to position text at the top, middle, or bottom of the line.

5. Mark the Word Wrap box if you want text to wrap automatically when it reaches the right margin of the text block.

6. Select the Frame button if you want to add a border or fill pattern to the text box (for details, see "Adding a Text Block Border and Pattern" in Lesson 5).

7. Select the Spacing & Indents button to configure spacing and indents. The Spacing & Indents dialog box appears (see Figure 6.4). Adjust the settings as necessary, and click on OK. You are returned to the Paragraph Styles box.

Spacing & Indents	?

1. Choose the paragraph style you want to change:

⊙ All   ○ 2nd   ▪ Level 1   **OK**
○ 1st   ○ 3rd   ▪ Level 2   **Cancel**
                ▸ Level 3

2. Set spacing and indents:

Spacing		Indents	
Paragraph:	1.15 ±	First line:	Mixed
Line:	1 (single) ±	Left:	0.0
		Right:	0.0

Figure 6.4   The Spacing & Indents dialog box.

Creating a Hanging Indent   If you want to format a style to have a hanging indent (where every line after the first line is indented), make the **Left** indent number greater than the **First line** number. For example, enter 10.0 next to **Left** and set the **First** line to 0.0.

8. Mark the Apply to SmartMaster check box if you want your changes to apply to every page in your presentation using the current page layout. For example, if you are modifying a text block on a page using the 2-Column Bullets page layout, all text blocks on other pages in your presentation using the 2-Column Bullets page layout will have the same characteristics.

9. If you wish to preview your changes, hold down the left mouse button on the Preview button until the sample appears. Release the mouse button to return to the dialog box.

10. If you want to undo all formatting changes you have made thus far and return the text to its original configuration, mark the Reset to SmartMaster check box.

11. Select OK. Freelance Graphics applies all formatting changes to corresponding text blocks.

In this lesson, you learned how to change the attributes of selected text and paragraph styles. In the next lesson, you will learn how to add new pages to your presentation.

Lesson 7

Using the Outliner

In this lesson, you will learn how to use the Outliner to develop a presentation.

Displaying the Outliner

Wouldn't it be frustrating if you had to work with your entire presentation one page at a time? Fortunately, the Outliner lets you see your entire presentation at once in outline form. This helps you to quickly create or edit the textual structure of your presentation.

You can display the Outliner at any point in the development of your presentation. You can create your entire presentation using the Outliner, or you can switch to the Outliner to edit a first draft of your presentation. To display the Outliner, do one of the following:

- Click on the Outliner icon located at the right side of the application window.

- Open the View menu, and select Outliner.

After switching to the Outliner, the appearance of your screen changes markedly. If you switch to the Outliner after you have started a presentation, your screen will resemble the configuration in Figure 7.1 (if you haven't yet begun a presentation, your screen will resemble Figure 7.2). Review Figure 7.1 to learn about the different components of the Outliner.

The Page icon indicates a presentation page.

The page title appears next to the Page icon.

Current Page icon

Page number

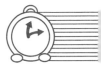

```
                Freelance Graphics - [BOARDMTG.PRE]      Ready
  File   Edit  View  Page  Outline  Style  Tools  Window  Help
                        Page 4
  [toolbar icons]  B  I  N       [icons]

  8 ▢ │ Winter Specials, Europe
              • Paris
                ▪ 10 day
                ▪ 21 day
              • London
                ▪ 10 day
                ▪ 21 day
  9 ▢ │ Winter Specials, South America
              • Rio de Janiero
                ▪ 14 day
                ▪ 21 day
              • Sao Paulo
                ▪ 14 day
                ▪ 21 day
              • Buenos Aires
                ▪ 10 day
                ▪ 21 day

  Outliner      Page Layout...  New Page...
```

Page number   Page icon   Level 2   Level 1   Outline icon

Figure 7.1   Components of the Outliner.

Starting in Outliner View   If you plan to draft most of your presentations in the Outliner, you can configure Freelance Graphics to start in Outliner view. Open the Tools menu, and select the User Setup menu. Select the Startup View Outliner option, and then OK.

To close the Outliner and return to the regular view for the current page (that is, the page currently selected in the Outliner), do one of the following:

• Click on the Current Page icon located at the right side of the application window.

• Open the View menu, and select Current Page.

Creating a Presentation in the Outliner

The Outliner is a good place to create a presentation, especially if that presentation includes many bulleted lists, or if you're still not sure about the presentation's format or order. It's easy to create new pages, rearrange bullets or pages, or rework the entire format of your presentation in the Outliner. To create a presentation in the Outliner, complete the following steps:

1. Create a new file (either by clicking on the File New icon, or by opening the File menu and selecting New).

2. Click on the Outliner icon, or open the View menu and select Outliner. The Outliner is displayed, as shown in Figure 7.2.

3. Type a title for your presentation next to the Page 1 icon, and then press Enter. The cursor moves to the next line.

4. Type the presentation subtitle, and then press Enter.

5. Click on the Promote icon (left arrow), or press Shift+Tab to create the next page in your presentation. Freelance Graphics always uses the Bulleted List page layout for each new page except the first.

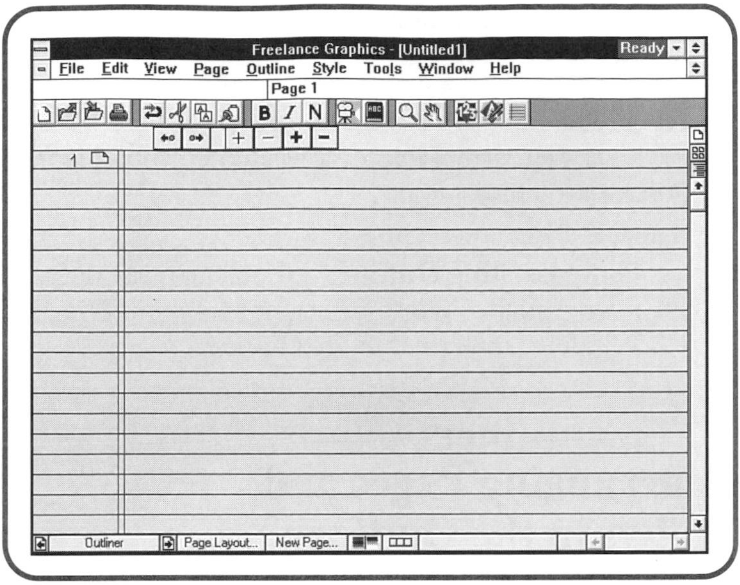

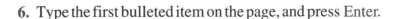

Figure 7.2   Creating a new presentation in the Outliner.

Using a Different Page Layout You might want to use a chart, table, or basic page layout instead of the bulleted list layout automatically assigned to each new page in the Outliner. To use a different page layout, make sure the cursor rests on any line of the page you want to change, and then select the Page Layout button at the bottom of the window. Or open the Page menu, and select Choose Page Layout. Select the page layout of your choice and then click on OK.

6. Type the first bulleted item on the page, and press Enter.

7. Continue entering text, using the Promote and Demote icons to order bullets and create new pages. Click on the

43

Page icon if you want to see what that page looks like in full view.

8. After you have finished drafting your presentation, click on the Page Sorter icon to view all of your presentation pages at once.

Using Existing Outlines   You can paste outlines from Ami Pro, WordPerfect, or Microsoft Word for Windows directly into the Outliner.

Rearranging Pages and Bullets in the Outliner

You can quickly move a single page or bullet, or more than one page or bullet in a row. To move a page, drag the Page icon (located to the right of the page number) to a new position. If you want to move a bulleted item, drag the bullet to a new position.

To move one or more pages or bullets to a new location, perform the following steps:

1. Click on the first page or bullet to select it.

2. Click the right mouse button on all subsequent pages or bullets you want to move (they must be contiguous). Freelance Graphics draws a box around the selected items, as shown in Figure 7.3.

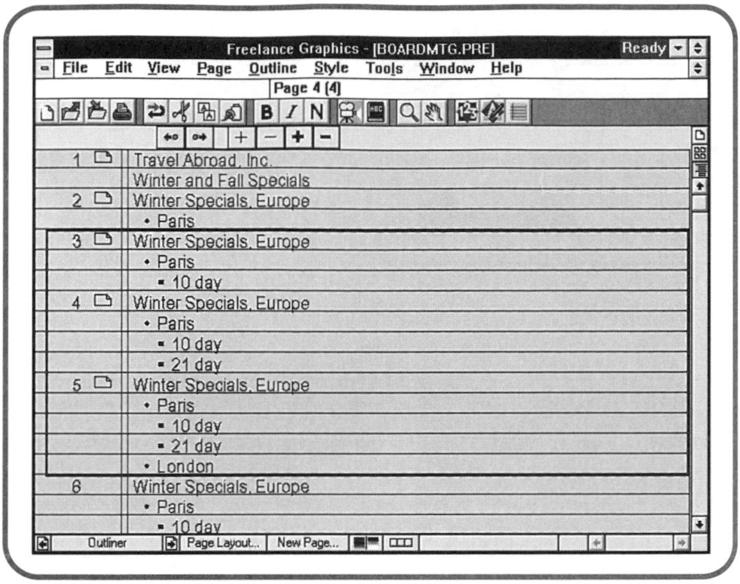

Figure 7.3   Selecting multiple pages and bullets.

3. Click anywhere on the selection (with the left mouse button). Drag it to its new location, and then release the mouse button. Freelance Graphics moves the items to their new location.

In this lesson, you learned how to use the Outliner to develop your presentation. In the next lesson, you will learn how to use the Page Sorter.

Organizing Pages with the Page Sorter

In this lesson, you will learn how to use the Page Sorter to rearrange, add, delete, and copy your presentation pages.

Switching to the Page Sorter

Managing your presentation is easy when you use the Page Sorter. The Page Sorter shows a small picture of each page in your presentation (see Figure 8.1). This makes it easy to reorganize your entire presentation, either by rearranging the page order, adding new pages, deleting pages, or copying pages.

To switch to the Page Sorter, click on the Page Sorter icon located at the right side of the window (see Figure 8.1), or open the View menu, and select Page Sorter. Freelance Graphics switches you from Current Page view to Page Sorter view, displaying a small picture of each presentation page as shown in Figure 8.1. A selection box borders the currently selected page.

Current Page icon

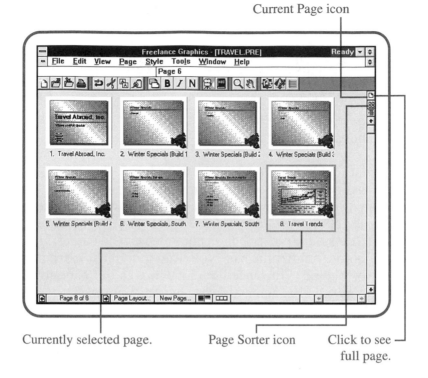

Currently selected page.   Page Sorter icon   Click to see full page.

Figure 8.1   Miniature presentation pages appear in Page Sorter view.

When you want to return to Current Page view, click on the Current Page icon (see Figure 8.1).

A Quick Switch   If you want to take a quick look at any one of your presentation pages in full view, double-click on that page. When you have finished reviewing the page, click on the Page Sorter icon again to return to Page Sorter view.

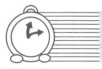

Rearranging the Page Order

It's easy to rearrange your presentation pages in Page Sorter view. To move a page to a new location, perform the following steps:

1. Select the page you want to move. A selection box borders the page.

2. Hold down the mouse button and drag the page to its new location. A vertical bar appears between pages as you drag to show you where the page will be inserted.

3. Release the mouse button once the vertical bar rests just before or after the page you want to move it in front of or behind. Freelance Graphics moves the page to its new location and assigns a new page number.

 **Moving Multiple Pages** To move a group of pages, hold down the Shift key as you click on each page you want to move. Then drag the pages to their new location.

Adding Pages

To add a new page to your presentation in Page Sorter view, perform the following steps:

1. Select the page which will precede the new page.

2. Select the New Page box at the bottom of the window, or open the Page menu, and select New. The New Page dialog box appears.

3. Select the page layout you want, and then select OK. The new page is inserted immediately after the currently selected page.

Deleting Pages

In order to delete an entire presentation page in Freelance Graphics, you must use the Page Sorter. To delete a page, perform the following steps:

1. Select the page you want to delete.

2. Open thePage menu, and select Remove, or press Delete.

I Deleted the Wrong Page!   If you realize that you deleted the wrong page right away, don't panic. Simply open the Edit menu, and select Undo. Freelance Graphics lets you undo the last ten actions you performed.

Copying Pages

You can copy an entire presentation page and use it in the same presentation or in another presentation.

To copy a page in the same presentation in Page Sorter view, perform the following steps:

1. Select the page you want to copy.

2. Open the **P**age menu, and select **D**uplicate. Freelance Graphics inserts a duplicate to the right of the page.

When you copy a page to a different presentation, the contents and layout of the copied page are duplicated in the new presentation page; however, Freelance Graphics uses the SmartMaster set assigned to the new presentation rather than the original presentation's set. To copy a page to another presentation, follow these steps:

1. Select the page you want to copy.

2. Open the **E**dit menu, and select **C**opy.

3. Open the presentation to which you want to copy the page (using the **F**ile **O**pen menu command).

4. Open the **E**dit menu, and select **P**aste. Freelance Graphics inserts the contents and layout of the copied page into a new page using the SmartMaster set assigned to the current presentation.

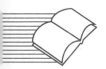 **The Windows Clipboard** The Clipboard is a temporary storage area that holds text you have cut or copied. Since all Windows applications share the same Clipboard, you can move text from any Windows application to another.

In this lesson, you learned how to rearrange, add, delete, and copy presentation pages using the Page Sorter. In the next lesson, you will learn how to create a title page and a bulleted list.

Lesson 9

Creating a Title Page, Bulleted List, and Build Pages

In this lesson, you will learn how to create a title page, bulleted list page, and build pages.

Creating a Title Page

A title page is the first page of the presentation that your audience sees. It is important to keep your title page simple and clear to create a good first impression. The SmartMaster set you chose when you were creating your presentation includes a predesigned title page. You can use the pre-set text boxes to enter your title, create your own text boxes, or add a symbol to the title page.

To create a title page for an existing presentation, follow these steps:

1. Use the File Open command to open the presentation if it is not already open.

2. Select New Page from the Page menu, or click on the New Page icon at the bottom of the screen.

3. The New Page dialog box appears. Select Title from the list box, and choose OK.

4. The title page appears on-screen (see Figure 9.1). Select any of the Click here . . . boxes to add text or symbols. (See Lesson 5 if you need help entering text.)

For a New Presentation If you are creating a new presentation, follow the directions in Lesson 2. When you come to the Choose Page Layout dialog box, select Title from the list box, then choose OK.

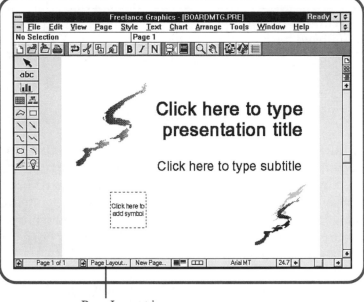

Page Layout icon

Figure 9.1 The title page.

If you are adding text boxes to your title page, be careful not to make the page look cramped. The title page should only list the title of your presentation and a subtitle (if needed). The body of your presentation will be in bulleted lists, charts and tables. Charts and tables are best for grouping information or comparing data. If you want to stress certain points or make a list, use a bulleted list.

Creating a Bulleted List

If you want to include a bulleted list in your presentation, you have four layouts from which to choose: a regular bulleted list, a two-column bulleted list, a bulleted list accompanied by a chart, and a bulleted list accompanied by a graphic symbol. To create a bulleted list, perform the following steps:

1. Open the Page menu, and select New; or click on the New Page icon at the bottom of the window. The New Page dialog box appears.

2. Select Bulleted List. A sample of the Bulleted List page layout displays in the right corner of the dialog box.

3. Select OK. Freelance Graphics displays a new page with the Bulleted List format.

4. Select the prompt text Click here to type page title. A text block opens.

5. Type a title for your page.

6. Select Click here to type bulleted text. A new text block opens.

7. Type the text for your first bulleted item, and press Enter. Freelance Graphics adds the next bullet automatically.

8. Continue to type bullet text, pressing Enter after you've typed each bullet. Follow these guidelines to achieve certain results:

   • To create a *sub-bullet*: Click on the Demote icon (right arrow), or press Tab.

- To return to the previous bullet level: Click on the Promote icon (left arrow), or press Shift+Tab.

- To type text on the next line without adding a bullet, press Ctrl+Enter.

9. Select OK, or press Esc when you finish typing all bullets. Your page structure should look something like the page in Figure 9.2.

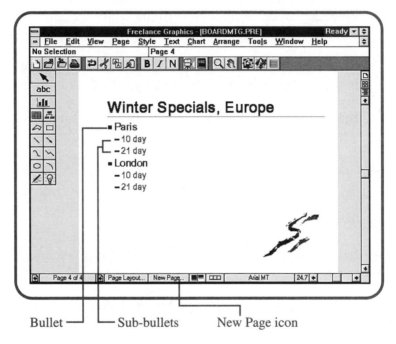

Bullet ──────── └─── Sub-bullets   New Page icon

Figure 9.2   The completed bulleted list.

Deleting a Bullet   If you want to delete a bullet but leave the text next to it intact, select the text next to the bullet and then open the Text menu, and select Bullet. When the Text Bullet dialog box appears, select None in the Style drop-down box, and then select OK.

Creating Build Pages

People usually lecture awhile on each point included in a bulleted list. You can strengthen the performance of your presentation by using a *build* for your bulleted list.

A build is a sequence of pages that lead up to the final point on the bulleted list. Freelance Graphics automatically creates as many build pages as necessary. The first page of the build displays the first bulleted item alone. The second page shows the next bulleted item, with the first item dimmed, and so on, until the list is complete. The original bulleted list becomes the final page in the build, with the last bullet in bold and all other bullets dimmed. To create a build, follow these steps:

1. Create a bulleted list following the instructions in the previous section. You can use any of the page layouts which have a bulleted list.

2. Open the Page menu, and select Create Build. Freelance Graphics creates the build pages for you automatically.

3. To view each page simultaneously, click on the Page Sorter icon at the right side of the application window. Then, to return to regular mode, click on the Current Page icon located just above the Page Sorter icon.

In this lesson, you learned how to create a title page, a bulleted list and build pages. In the next lesson, you will learn how to create a pie chart.

Creating a Pie Chart

This lesson shows you how to create and edit a pie chart.

About Charts

Charts can really enhance a presentation. You may think charting involves hard work and lots of hours, but with Freelance Graphics, creating a chart is easy and quick. You just choose a chart type and style and then enter your data. What you end up with is a truly professional-looking, sophisticated chart.

Freelance Graphics provides templates for many types of charts, including pie, bar, line, high-low-open-close, and organization charts. This lesson teaches you how to create a pie chart. Lessons 11 through 14 show you how to create the other types of charts.

Creating a Pie Chart

Use a pie chart if you want to display the sizes of parts of a whole set of data. Each slice of the pie represents a percentage of the total data set. To create a pie chart, perform the following steps:

1. Open the **P**age menu, and select New, or click on the New Page box at the bottom of the window. The New Page dialog box appears.

2. Select the chart page layout you want.

3. Select OK. Freelance Graphics creates a new page using the chart layout you specified.

4. Select Click here to type page title, and type a title for this page.

5. Select Click here to create chart. The New Chart Gallery dialog box appears, as seen in Figure 10.1.

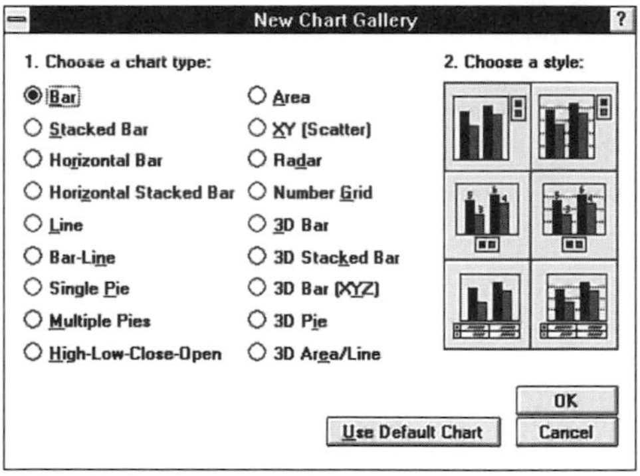

Figure 10.1 The New Chart Gallery displays all chart types and styles.

6. Select the chart type you want. Each of the three types comes in various styles. The available styles for the chart type you choose are displayed on the right side of the dialog box.

7. Select the style you want. The Chart Data & Titles dialog box appears, as shown in Figure 10.2.

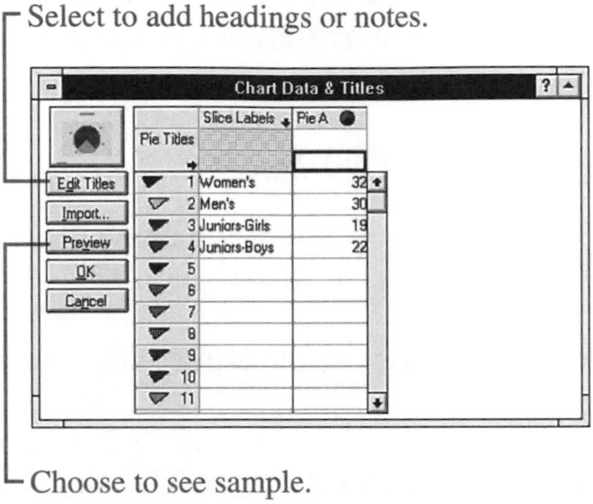

Select to add headings or notes.

Choose to see sample.

Figure 10.2   Enter your data in the Chart Data & Titles dialog box.

8. Enter the axis labels, legend labels, and chart data in the spreadsheet area of the Chart Data & Titles dialog box. Freelance Graphics uses this information to draw your chart.

9. To enter a heading, notes, or axis titles, select the Edit Titles button on the left side of the dialog box. The appearance of the Chart Data & Titles dialog box changes (see Figure 10.3).

10. Next to Headings, type up to three lines for a chart heading. Any text you type here will be placed below the page title you entered in step 4 (see Figure 10.4).

11. If you want to include any notes, type them in the box next to Notes. You can type up to three lines of notes. Freelance Graphics places the notes (formatted in a

small point size) at the bottom left of the chart. This is an ideal place to cite sources used for the chart.

Select to return to spreadsheet.

	Chart Data & Titles	?	▲

Headings: Quarterly Report - Fall 1993

NAPA

Edit Data

Import...

Preview

OK

Cancel

Notes: Source: R.R. Jay Consultants

Select to see sample.

Figure 10.3 Enter headings or notes in this dialog box.

12. To preview your chart, hold down the mouse button on the Preview button until an illustration of the chart displays. Release the mouse button and make changes to the chart data or titles if necessary.

13. Select OK. Freelance Graphics draws your chart to fit into the confines of the Click here . . . chart block on the page (see Figure 10.4).

Importing Data from Another Source One of the best aspects of the Freelance Graphics charting feature is that you can import data from other files and Windows-based spreadsheet applications (such as 1-2-3, Excel, or Quattro Pro for Windows) directly into the worksheet area of the Chart Data & Titles dialog box. For details, refer to the Freelance Graphics for Windows documentation that accompanies your software.

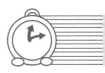

59

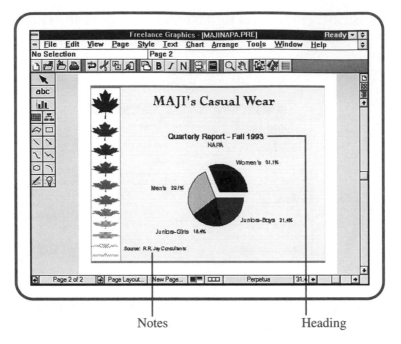

Notes   Heading

Figure 10.4   The completed pie chart.

Editing a Pie Chart

After creating a pie chart, you can change its appearance or data following these steps:

1. Select the pie. The Pie Chart Attributes dialog box appears, as shown in Figure 10.5.

2. Select the slice you want to change. If you are working with multiple pies, the corresponding slice in each pie will be modified.

Select to see sample.

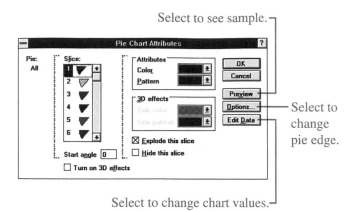

Select to change chart values.

Select to change pie edge.

Figure 10.5 The Pie Chart Attributes dialog box.

Slicing the Pie Slices are numbered counterclockwise, beginning at the 3 o'clock position. If you want to change the angle of the slices (so that the first slice starts at 1 o'clock, for example), enter a new number in the Start angle box. For instance, to start the first slice at 1 o'clock, you would enter 60 for 60 degrees.

3. From the Pie Chart Attributes dialog box, you can:

   • Make changes to the Attributes and 3D Effects boxes.

   • Select the Options button if you want to apply changes to the edge of the pie or to configure additional 3D settings.

   • Mark the Explode this slice check box to make the slice stand out from the rest of the pie.

- Mark the Hide this slice to make the slice invisible.

- Select the Edit Data button to change chart figures.

- Hold down the mouse button on the Preview button to see how your changes look. Release the mouse button to return to the dialog box.

4. Select OK when you are done editing your pie chart. Freelance Graphics automatically applies the changes to your chart.

5. Open the File menu and select Save to save your new chart.

This lesson showed you how to create and edit a pie chart. In the next lesson, you will learn how create and edit a bar chart.

Lesson 11

Creating a Bar Chart

This lesson shows you how to create and edit a bar chart.

About Bar Charts

While pie charts are useful to emphasize components of a whole data set, bar charts are good to use when working with several data sets. Use a bar chart when you want to compare a category's data in relation to units. For example, as in the chart in Figure 11.3, a bar chart may show the dollar amount (units) sold for certain types of clothing (data sets) at various department store sites (categories).

Data Set   A data set is a set of values for one category. Each bar represents a data set in a bar chart.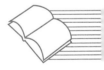

Like the bar chart shown in Figure 11.3, units are usually displayed on the vertical y-axis and categories on the horizontal x-axis. Data sets represented by different bars are identified in a legend.

Creating a Bar Chart

To create a bar chart, select the Click here to create chart box. The New Chart Gallery dialog box will appear. From this dialog box, select a bar chart as the chart type, and select the style of chart you want. The Chart Data & Titles dialog box will appear, as shown in Figure 11.1

Enter X-axis labels in this column.

Enter Legend text in this row.

Choose to see sample.

Select to add headings, notes, or axes titles.

Figure 11.1 The Chart Data & Titles dialog box with sample entries.

To finish creating the bar chart, perform the following steps:

1. Enter the legend names in the Legend area of the chart. A legend name tells you the data set associated with a bar.

2. Enter the x-axis labels in the Axis Labels column.

3. Enter values in the main worksheet area. Freelance Graphics automatically sets up the y-axis labels based on the values in the worksheet.

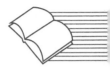

Axis Labels and Titles   Axis labels identify the information being charted, while axis titles identify or summarize the axis labels. (For example, you may use an axis title of "Dollars" to identify the numbers appearing on the Y-axis.)

4. To enter a heading, notes, or axis titles, select the Edit Titles button on the left side of the dialog box. The appearance of the Chart Data & Titles dialog box changes, as shown in Figure 11.2.

Select to return to spreadsheet.

Choose to see sample.

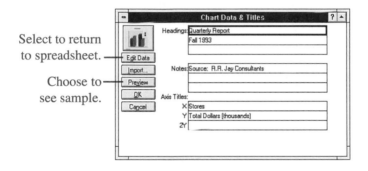

Figure 11.2   Enter headings, notes, and axes titles in this portion of the dialog box.

5. Next to Headings, type up to three lines for a chart heading. Any text you type here will be placed below the page title (see Figure 11.3).

6. If you want to include notes, type them in the box next to Notes. You can type up to three lines of notes. Freelance Graphics places the notes (in a small point size) at the bottom left of the chart. This is an ideal place to cite sources used for the chart (see Figure 11.3).

7. If you want to title either of the axes, type the titles in the boxes next to the X or Y in the Axis Titles section.

Freelance Graphics places the Y-axis title immediately above the top Y-axis heading, and centers the X-axis title just below the chart (see Figure 11.3).

8. To preview your chart, hold down the mouse button over the Preview button until an illustration of the chart displays. Release the mouse button to return to the dialog box.

9. Select OK. Freelance Graphics draws your chart to fit into the Click here . . . chart block on the presentation page (see Figure 11.3).

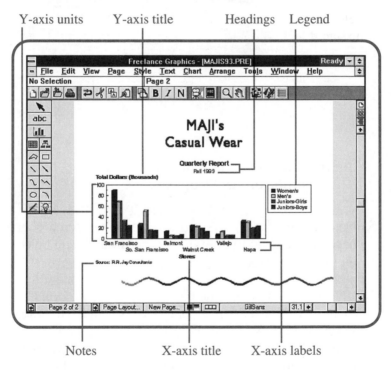

Figure 11.3 The completed bar chart.

Editing a Bar Chart

After creating a bar chart, you can change its appearance or data following these steps:

1. Select the bar chart. The Bar Chart Attributes dialog box appears, as shown in Figure 11.4

No Results   If you select a bar chart and nothing happens, this means the chart was previously selected. Select a blank area of the page, and then click on the bar chart again to display the Bar Chart Attributes dialog box.

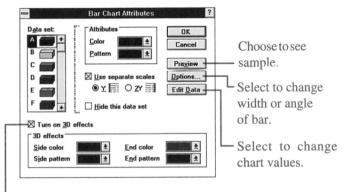

Choose to see sample.

Select to change width or angle of bar.

Select to change chart values.

Check to add units on right side of chart.

Figure 11.4   The Bar Chart Attributes dialog box.

2. Select the data set (bar) you want to change.

3. Make changes to the Attributes and 3D Effects boxes, if you want.

4. Select the Options button if you want to change the width or angle of the bar or to alter the percentage of 3D effects.

67

5. Mark the Use separate scales check box if you want to use two scaled Y-axes. Then choose which axis (the Y- or 2Y-axis) you want to use for this bar.

6. Mark the Hide this data set to make the bar invisible.

7. Select the Edit Data button to change chart values.

8. Hold down the mouse button on the Preview button to see how your changes look. Release the mouse button to return to the dialog box.

9. Select OK. Freelance Graphics applies the changes to the bar chart.

In this lesson, you learned how to create and edit a bar chart. The next lesson teaches you how to create and edit a line chart.

Creating a Line Chart

This lesson shows you how to create and edit a line chart.

About Line Charts

Like bar charts, line charts use X- and Y-axes to present information on data sets. Since line charts generally stress the continuity of data over time, create a line chart to make projections, to present data that shows trends, or to demonstrate how data set values change over time.

Creating a Line Chart

To create a chart, select the Click here to create chart box. The New Chart Gallery dialog box will appear. From this dialog box, select a line chart as the chart type, and select the style of chart you want. The Chart Data & Titles dialog box will appear, as shown in Figure 12.1.

Select to add headings, notes, or axes titles.

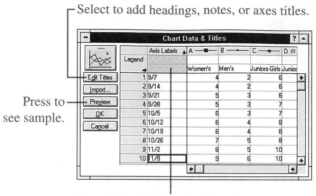

Press to see sample.

Enter X-axis labels in this column.

Figure 12.1 The Chart Data & Titles dialog box with sample entries.

To continue creating a line chart, perform the following steps:

1. Enter the legend names in the Legend area of the chart. A legend name tells you which data set a line represents.

2. Enter the X-axis labels in the Axis Labels column. X-axis labels usually represent time periods; for example, the chart in Figure 12.2 displays weekly dates on the X-axis.

3. Enter values in the main worksheet area. Freelance Graphics automatically sets up the Y-axis labels based on the values in the worksheet.

4. To enter a heading, notes, or axis titles, select the Edit Titles button on the left side of the dialog box. The appearance of the Chart Data & Titles dialog box changes.

5. Next to Headings, type up to three lines for a chart heading. Any text you type here will be placed below the page title (see Figure 12.2).

6. If you want to include notes, type them in the box next to Notes. You can type up to three lines of notes. Freelance Graphics places the notes (in a small point size) at the bottom left of the chart. This is an ideal place to cite sources used for the chart (see Figure 12.2).

7. If you want to title either of the axes, type the titles in the boxes next to the X or Y in the Axis Titles section. Freelance Graphics places the Y-axis title immediately above the top Y-axis heading and centers the X-axis title just below the chart (see Figure 12.2).

8. To preview your chart, hold down the mouse button over the Preview button until an illustration of the chart displays. Release the mouse button to return to the dialog box.

9. Click on OK twice. Freelance Graphics draws your chart to fit into the Click here . . . chart block on the presentation page (see Figure 12.2).

Applying 3D to Your Line Chart   To apply 3D effects to a regular line chart after it has been created, hold down the right mouse button on the chart until a menu appears, and then select Gallery. Select the 3D Area/Line, and then select the style you want. Freelance Graphics applies 3D effects to the existing chart.

71

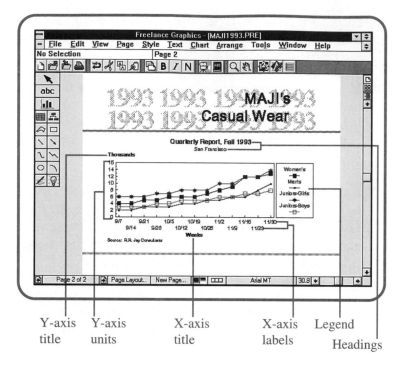

Figure 12.2   The completed line chart.

Editing a Line Chart

After creating a line chart, you can change its appearance or data following these steps:

1. Select the chart.

2. Open the Chart menu, and select Attributes. The Line Chart Attributes dialog box appears, as shown in Figure 12.3.

3. Select the Data set (line) you want to change.

4. Change the color, width, or style of the line in the Attributes box.

5. Select a new marker in the Attributes box. If you don't want markers showing in your chart, select None in the Marker drop-down box.

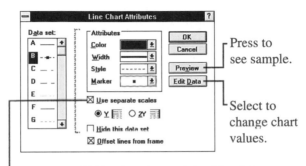

Figure 12.3 The Line Chart Attributes dialog box.

What Is a Marker? A line represents a data set, and each marker on that line represents one value of the data set at a particular time. Markers point out where the X- and Y-axis items meet.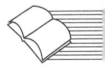

6. Mark the Use separate scales check box if you want to use two scaled Y-axes. Then choose which axis (the Y- or 2Y-axis) you want to use for this line.

7. Mark the Hide this data set to make the line invisible.

8. Unmark the Offset lines from frame check box to display lines at the beginning of the frame.

9. Select the Edit Data button to change chart values.

10. Hold down the mouse button on the Preview button to see how your changes look. Release the mouse button to return to the dialog box.

11. Select OK. Freelance Graphics applies the changes to the line chart.

In this lesson, you learned how to create and edit a line chart. The next lesson teaches you how to create and edit a high-low-close-open chart.

Lesson 13

Creating a High-Low-Close-Open Chart

This lesson shows you how to create and edit a high-low-close-open (HLCO) chart.

About HLCO Charts

HLCO charts, sometimes called Stock Market charts, are generally used to illustrate stock performance, though they can track any data that fluctuates over a period of time, such as currency rates. These charts plot four data sets: the high, low, closing, and opening prices of a stock (or another item). You don't need to include all four data sets in your chart. For example, the chart in Figure 13.2 tracks only high and low values.

An HLCO chart displays each set of values as a vertical line with tick marks. The top of the line shows the high value and the bottom of the line shows the low value.

Tick Marks   Tick marks are short lines that indicate a point on the X- or Y-axis. A tick mark on the left side of the line marks the opening value, while a tick mark on the right side of the line indicates the closing value.

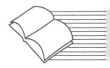

Creating a HLCO Chart

To create an HLCO chart, first select the Click here to create chart box. The New Chart Gallery dialog box will appear. From this dialog box, select the High-Low-Close-Open chart as the chart type, and then select the style of chart you want. The Chart Data & Titles dialog box will appear, as shown in Figure 13.1

Select to add   Enter X-axis labels in this column.
headings,
notes, or
axes titles.

Choose to
see sample.

Figure 13.1   The Chart Data & Titles dialog box, with sample entries.

To finish creating the chart, perform these steps:

1. Freelance Graphics automatically enters the legend names for you. However, if you want to make the names more specific, type over the current names.

2. Enter the X-axis labels in the Axis Labels column. X-axis labels usually represent time periods; for example, days of the week are displayed on the X-axis of the chart in Figure 13.2.

76

3. Enter values in the main worksheet area. Freelance Graphics automatically sets up the Y-axis labels based on the values in the worksheet.

4. To enter a heading, notes, or axis titles, select the Edit Titles button on the left side of the dialog box. The appearance of the Chart Data & Titles dialog box changes.

5. Next to Headings, type up to three lines for a chart heading. Any text you type here will be placed below the page title.

6. If you want to include notes, type them in the box next to Notes. You can type up to three lines of notes. Freelance Graphics places the notes (in a small point size) at the bottom left of the chart. This is an ideal place to cite sources used for the chart.

7. If you want to title either of the axes, type the titles in the boxes next to the X and Y in the Axis Titles section. Freelance Graphics places the Y-axis title immediately above the top Y-axis unit ("Customers" in Figure 13.2), and centers the X-axis title just below the chart.

8. To preview your chart, hold down the mouse button on the Preview button until an illustration of the chart appears. Release the mouse button to return to the dialog box.

9. Selct OK. Freelance Graphics draws your chart to fit into the Click here . . . chart block on the presentation page (see Figure 13.2).

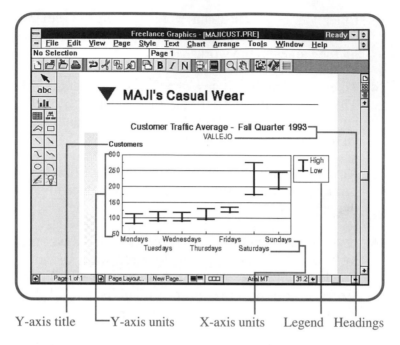

Y-axis title   └─Y-axis units   X-axis units   Legend   Headings

Figure 13.2   The completed HLCO chart.

Editing an HLCO Chart

After creating an HLCO chart, you can change its appearance or data following these steps:

1. Hold down the right mouse button on the chart until a menu appears and then select Attributes. The HLCO Chart Attributes dialog box appears, as shown in Figure 13.3.

2. Select the data set (vertical line or tick mark) you want to change.

Choose to see sample.

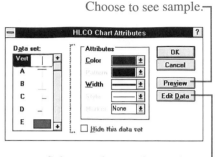

Select to change chart values.

Figure 13.3 The HLCO Chart Attributes dialog box.

3. Change the color or width of the line or tick mark in the Attributes box.

4. Mark the Hide this data set to make a tick mark invisible. You can only hide closing and opening tick marks.

5. Select the Edit Data button to change chart values.

6. Hold down the mouse button on the Preview button to see how your changes look. Release the mouse button to return to the dialog box.

7. Select OK. Freelance Graphics applies the changes to the line chart.

In this lesson, you learned how to create and edit a high-low-close-open chart. The next lesson teaches you how to create and edit an organization chart.

Creating an Organization Chart

In this lesson, you will learn how to create and edit an organization chart.

About Organization Charts

Organization charts are very different from data charts (pie, bar, line, and so on), though they are all called charts. The purpose of an organization chart is to show a hierarchy, not to track data trends. Organization charts are frequently used to map the staff structure of a company (see Figure 14.3).

Creating an Organization Chart

Creating an organization chart is different from creating a regular data chart. To create an organization chart, perform the following steps:

1. Open the Page menu, and select New; or click on the New Page icon at the bottom of the window. The New Page dialog box appears.

2. Select Organization Chart, and then OK. Freelance Graphics creates a new page with the Organization Chart page layout.

3. Select Click here to type page title, and type a title for this page.

4. Select Click here to create organization chart. The Organization Chart Gallery dialog box appears, as shown in Figure 14.1.

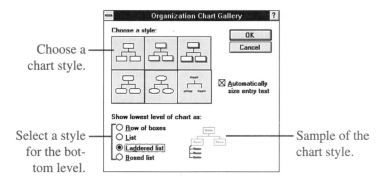

Figure 14.1   Select a style for your organization chart using this dialog box.

5. Click on the chart style of your choice.

6. Decide how you want the lowest level of the chart displayed, and then select the appropriate option.

7. Mark the Automatically size entry text check box if you want Freelance Graphics to let you type in as much text as you want into each box. If you want all entry text to be the same point size, clear this check box.

Too Small! A large organization chart often contains very small entry text. Experiment with different styles to find the one that makes best use of chart space. Certain fonts occupy less room, and attributes (such as boldface and italics) can also affect the overall size of text.

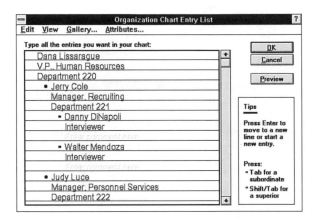

Figure 14.2 Enter the text for your chart in this dialog box.

8. Select OK. The Organization Chart Entry List dialog box appears (see Figure 14.2).

9. Enter the information for your first level entry where the entry list prompt text tells you to type. You can type up to three lines per entry. Even if an entry contains only one line of text, you must press Enter from the third line of that entry in order to move to the next one.

10. Type the second level entry (there can only be one entry at the top level). If you want this entry to be a support staff entry (reporting directly to the top), open the dialog box Edit menu, and select Staff *before* you start typing.

11. Create the rest of the chart entries following the guidelines in Table 14.1.

12. You can preview a sample of the chart, and then select OK. Freelance Graphics draws the chart so that it fits into the chart block on the presentation page, as seen in Figure 14.3.

Table 14.1   Organizing the Chart Entries.

To achieve this result:	Do the following:
Type an entry at the same level.	Type the new entry.
Type a subordinate entry at the next level.	Press Tab before typing the entry.
Type a superior entry at the previous (higher) level.	Press Shift+Tab before typing the entry.

Deleting an Entry   To delete an entry, select the bullet next to the first line of the entry, and press the Delete key.

Editing an Organization Chart

Organization charts can be modified in several ways. You can change the attributes of text or boxes for a single entry, levels of the chart, or the entire chart. You can also modify the color, width, and styles of the connecting lines, or apply a border and fill pattern to the frame holding the chart. To edit an organization chart, perform the following steps:

1. Click anywhere on the chart to select it.

2. Select any one of the boxes. The Organization Chart Attributes dialog box appears, as shown in Figure 14.4.

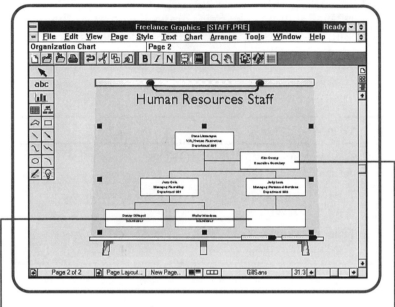

Click here to enter text directly.   Create this box with Edit Staff.

Figure 14.3   The completed organization chart.

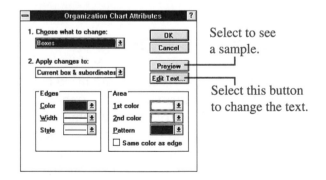

Select to see a sample.

Select this button to change the text.

Figure 14.4   The Organization Chart Attributes dialog box.

3. Choose the item to change from the drop-down list. The options in the dialog box change depending on what item you chose.

4. If you are modifying text or boxes, specify where to apply the changes by using the drop-down list of areas to change.

5. Set the rest of the dialog box options.

6. To edit the chart text itself, select the Edit Text button. In the Organization Chart Entry List dialog box, change text as needed, and select OK.

Speeding It Up   To change text directly from the box, select the chart. Then select the box containing the text you want to change. The cursor moves inside the box; you are ready to add, change, or delete text.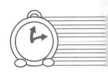

7. Hold the mouse down on the Preview button until a sample appears. Release the mouse button and make changes if necessary.

8. Select OK. Freelance Graphics applies all formatting changes to the organization chart.

In this lesson, you learned how to create and edit an organization chart. In the next lesson, you will learn how to create a table.

Creating a Table

In this lesson, you will learn how to create a table.

Creating a Table

Freelance Graphics makes it easy to use tables in your presentation. The best way to create a table is to use the Table page layout.

To create a new page containing a table, perform the following steps:

1. Open the Page menu and select New, or click on the New Page box located at the bottom of the window. The New Page dialog box appears.

2. Select the Table page layout. An illustration of the Table page layout appears in the dialog box.

3. Select OK. Freelance Graphics creates a new presentation page using the Table page layout.

4. Select the Click here to type page title prompt text, and type a title for this page.

5. Select the Click here to create table prompt text. The Table Gallery dialog box appears, as shown in Figure 15.1.

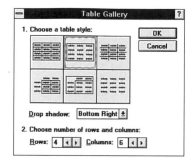

Figure 15.1   The Table Gallery dialog box.

6. Select the table style of your choice, following these guidelines:

Style 1   Draws a line around each cell in the table and a line around the edge of the entire table.

Style 2   Draws a line around the edge of the entire table.

Style 3   Draws a line around each cell of the table (but not around the edge of the table).

Style 4   Draws lines around each data cell in the table. Does not draw a line around the title cells.

Style 5   Draws a line around the edge of the table and a line separating the title cells from the data cells.

Style 6   Does not draw any lines.

7. If you want to add a drop shadow to the table, select the style you want in the **D**rop shadow box.

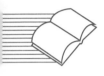

What Is a Drop Shadow? A drop shadow is a thick line that is added to the bottom right, bottom left, top right, or top left borders of the table. These lines are drawn in such a way that it appears a shadow rests behind the table (see Figure 15.2).

8. Enter the amount of rows you want in the **R**ows box. Use the arrow buttons to set the number, or move the insertion point into the box and type the number. Don't forget to include a row for the column headings.

9. Enter the amount of columns you want in the **C**olumns box. Use the arrow buttons to set the number, or move the insertion point into the box and type the number. Don't forget to include a column for the row headings.

10. Select OK. Freelance Graphics adds a table of the specified style and size to the page, as shown in Figure 15.2.

11. Press the Spacebar or F2; the insertion point moves into the first cell (upper-left corner for top-left corner) in the table. Type a label or data figure. To begin typing text in a cell other than the first, click on that cell rather than pressing the Spacebar or F2.

12. Type labels and data in the table cells. To start another line in the same cell, press Enter. To move to the next cell, press Tab. To move to the previous cell, press Shift+Tab. Alternatively, you can use the arrow keys to navigate through the table cells.

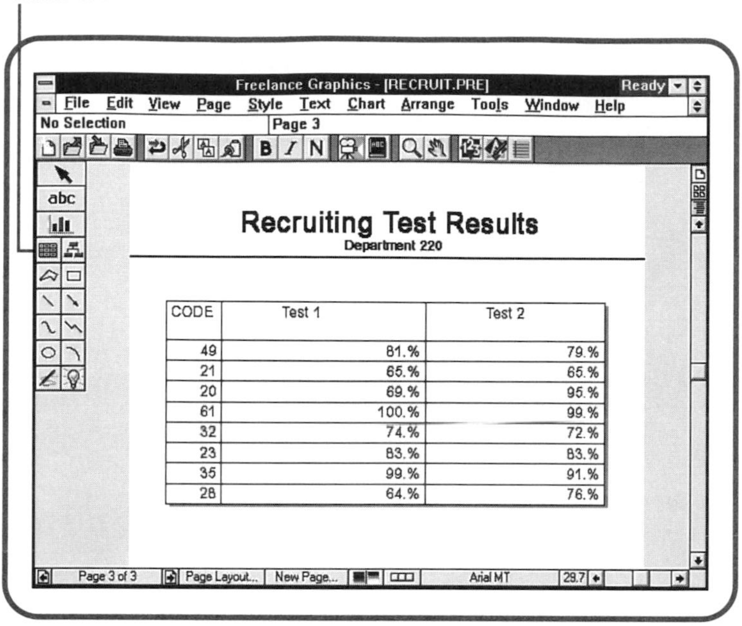

Table icon

Freelance Graphics - [RECRUIT.PRE] — Ready

File Edit View Page Style Text Chart Arrange Tools Window Help

No Selection | Page 3

abc

Recruiting Test Results

Department 220

CODE	Test 1	Test 2
49	81.%	79.%
21	65.%	65.%
20	69.%	95.%
61	100.%	99.%
32	74.%	72.%
23	83.%	83.%
35	99.%	91.%
28	64.%	76.%

Page 3 of 3 | Page Layout... | New Page... | | Arial MT | 29.7

Figure 15.2   Freelance Graphics adds the new table to the presentation page.

Adding a Table to Any Page   It isn't necessary to start a new page to create a table. You can add a table to any presentation page. Just open the Chart menu, select New and **Table**, or click on the Table icon in the Toolbox.

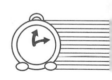

In this lesson, you learned how to create a table. In the next lesson, you will learn how to edit a table.

89

Lesson 16
Editing a Table

In this lesson, you will learn how to edit a table.

Changing Text and Table Attributes

You can modify text, line, and border attributes of single cells or an entire table. You can also resize, insert, delete, and move columns and rows in a table, as well as resize the table itself.

To modify text and table attributes, perform the following steps:

1. Select the portion of the table you want to edit, following the guidelines in Table 16.1.

Table 16.1   Selecting a table and parts of a table.

To:	Do the following (make sure the table isn't selected yet):
Select a table	Click the table once.
Select a cell	Click the table once to select it. Click the cell to enter edit mode, and then drag the mouse to highlight the cell.

90

To:	Do the following (make sure the table isn't selected yet):
Select characters in a cell	Click the table once to select it. Click the cell to enter edit mode, then drag the mouse over the characters.
Select a group of cells	Click the table once to select it. Click the first cell in the group to enter edit mode, and then drag the mouse to highlight all the cells.

2. Open the Chart menu, and select Attributes. The Table Attributes dialog box appears, as shown in Figure 16.1.

Choose to see sample.

Table Attributes

1. Choose what you want to change:
   - ⦿ Text Attributes
   - ○ Cell background & borders
   - ○ Table background & border

   OK
   Cancel
   Preview

2. Choose attributes:

   Font
   Face: Arial MT
   Size: 16.7
   Text color:

   ☒ Normal
   ☐ Bold
   ☐ Italic
   ☐ Underline
   ☐ Strikeout

   Text justification:

Figure 16.1   The Table Attributes dialog box.

Quick Editing   To quickly edit an entire table, double-click anywhere on the table to bring up the Table Attributes dialog box.

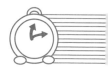

3. Select the item you want to change: text attributes or the background and border of selected cells or of the whole table. The appearance of the Table Attributes dialog box changes depending on your selection.

4. Change the attributes.

5. Hold the mouse button over the Preview button if you want to see a sample of what the table looks like with the new settings.

6. Select OK. Freelance Graphics makes the specified changes.

Modifying Rows, Columns, and Table Size

Youcan resize a column, row, or table, as well as insert, delete, and move columns and rows.

Resizing a Column, Row, or Table

To resize a column, row, or table, follow these steps:

1. Click on the table once to select it.

2. To resize a column or row, click on a cell to enter the edit mode. Then position the mouse pointer over the dividing line next to the column or row you want to change. When the pointer becomes a two-way arrow, drag the line in the direction you want it (see Figure 16.2). Release the mouse when the column or row is the right size.

Selection handle

Freelance Graphics - [RECRUIT.PRE]   Ready

File Edit View Page Style Text Chart Arrange Tools Window Help

Table   Page 3

Recruiting Test Results
Department 220

CODE	Test 1 - Written	Test 2 - Oral
49	81.%	79.%
21	65.%	65.%
20	69.%	95.%
61	100.%	99.%
32	74.%	72.%
23	83.%	83.%
35	99.%	91.%
28	64.%	76.%

Page 3 of 3   Page Layout...   New Page...   Arial MT   25.9

Figure 16.2   Resizing a column.

3. To resize the entire table, move the mouse over a
   selection handle until the pointer becomes a two-way
   arrow (see Figure 16.2). Hold down the mouse as you
   drag the handle in the desired direction. Repeat this step
   until the table is the size you want it.

Selection Handles   The little boxes that appear on
a frame containing a table, chart, or symbol when
the object is selected. In addition to letting you
know if an object is selected, selection handles can
be used to resize the frame.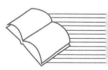

Inserting a Column or Row

To insert a column or row, perform these steps:

1. Click on the table once to select it.

2. Click on the row above the row you want to insert, or the column in front of the column you want to insert. Freelance Graphics will place the new row below the current row, or the new column after the current column.

3. Press the right mouse button to display a menu for the table (see Figure 16.3).

Figure 16.3   Press the right mouse button to display this menu.

4. Select Insert Column/Row. The Insert Column/Row dialog box appears, as shown in Figure 16.4.

5. Select Column or Row, depending on what you want to insert.

6. Select After. (Or if you want to insert a row above the current row or column before the current column, select Before.)

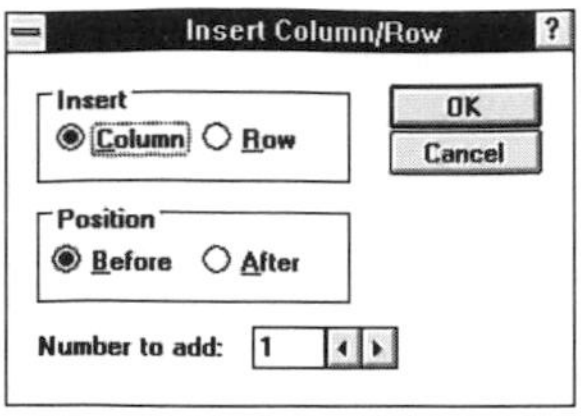

Figure 16.4   The Insert Column/Row dialog box.

7. To add more than one column or row, enter an amount in the box next to Number to add.

8. Select OK. Freelance Graphics inserts the new column(s) or row(s) into the table.

Deleting a Column or Row

Deleting Text Only   To delete only the text from a column or row, leaving the column or row intact, highlight the column or row and press Delete. The text disappears but the empty column or row remains.

To delete a column or row, perform these steps:

1. Click on the table once to select it.

2. Click on the row or column you want to delete.

3. Press the right mouse button to display a menu for the table (see Figure 16.3).

4. Select Delete Column/Row. The Delete Column/Row dialog box appears.

5. Select Column or Row, depending on what you want to delete.

6. Select OK. Freelance Graphics removes the column or row from the table.

I Deleted the Wrong Thing! If you accidentally delete the wrong column or row, open the Edit menu, and select Undo Col/Row Delete.

Moving a Column or Row

To move a column or row, follow these steps:

1. Click on the table once to select it.

2. Click on the row or column you want to move.

3. Press the right mouse button to display a menu for the table (see Figure 16.3).

4. Select Move Column/Row. The Move Column/Row dialog box appears, as shown in Figure 16.5.

5. Click on Column or Row, depending on what you want to move.

6. Specify the direction in which you want the column or row moved.

7. Click on OK. Freelance Graphics moves the column or row as specified.

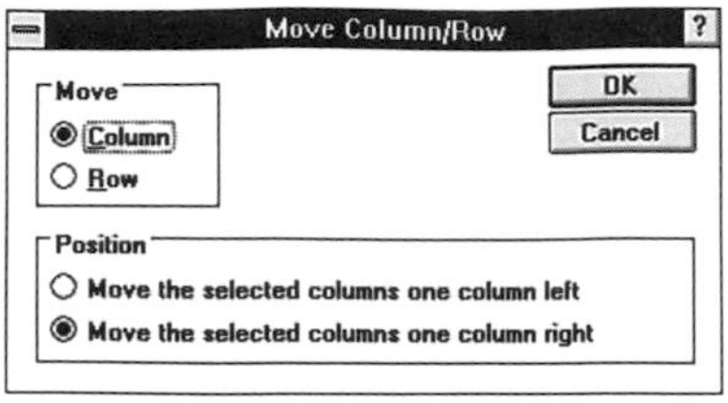

Figure 16.5   The Move Column/Row dialog box.

In this lesson, you learned how to edit a table. In the next lesson, you will learn how to add a symbol to your presentation.

Lesson 17

Printing Your Presentation

This lesson shows you how to print presentations, speaker notes, audience notes, handouts, and outlines.

Printing Your Presentation

You can print your presentation in color or in black and white, depending on the printers available for your use. Make sure to display your presentation in color if you want to print in color (on a color printer, of course). Read Lesson 21, "Changing the Look of your Presentation," for details on switching between color and black and white modes.

To print certain pages of your presentation or the entire presentation, perform the following steps:

 **Printing One Page** To print only one page, display that page on your screen before following the procedures below.

1. Open the File menu, and select Print, or press Ctrl+P. The Print File dialog box appears, as shown in Figure 17.1.

2. If you want to print more than one copy, type a new number next to **N**umber of copies.

3. To print only the page showing on your screen, mark the Current page only check box.

4. If you want to print only certain consecutive pages of your presentation, enter the numbers of the first and last pages in the From page and to boxes.

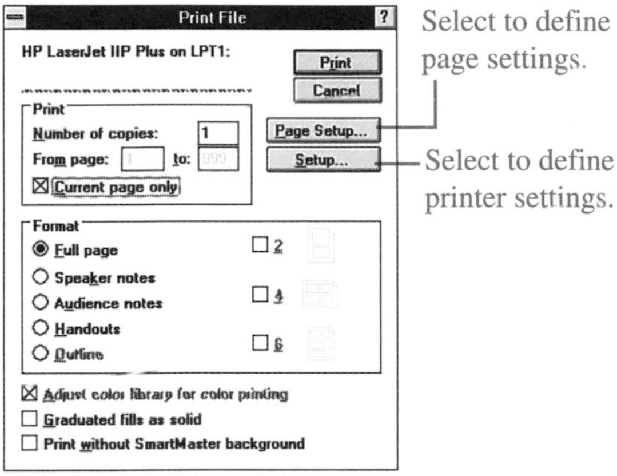

Select to define page settings.

Select to define printer settings.

Figure 17.1   The Print File dialog box.

Can I Print Nonconsecutive Pages?   You can print certain pages scattered throughout your presentation from the Page Sorter view. Select the pages you want to print by pressing Shift as you click on each page. Then open the File menu, select Print, and mark Selected pages only check box and select Print.

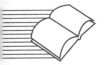 **Graduated Fills**   Patterns that gradually change from one color or design to another. If you print a graduated fill as a color, the pattern or color change does not appear.

5. Some printers cannot print graduated fills, so if you want to replace the graduated fills in your presentation with a solid color, mark the Graduated fills as solid check box.

6. If you want to print without using the graphics supplied by the SmartMaster set assigned to your presentation, mark the Print without SmartMaster background dialog box. Though the position of text and graphics does not change, the background design of the SmartMaster does not print.

7. Select the Page Setup button if you want to change the page setup and alter the appropriate settings in the Page Setup dialog box.

8. If you want to make changes to the printer setup, click on the Setup button and modify the appropriate settings in the Printer Setup dialog box.

9. Select the Print button. Freelance Graphics prints your presentation as specified.

Printing Speaker Notes, Audience Notes, Handouts, and Outlines

To print speaker notes, audience notes, handouts, and outlines, follow the procedures outlined above but choose the appropriate item in the Format box of the Print File dialog box. Here is what will be printed when you select the following items:

Speaker notes   Freelance Graphics places the presentation page on the top half of the printed page and the speaker notes on the bottom half of the printed page.

Audience notes   Freelance Graphics places the presentation page on the top half of the printed page and blank lines on the bottom half of the printed page. This format is ideal to use if you expect members of your audience to take notes during the presentation.

Handouts   Freelance Graphics places two, four, or six presentation pages on each printed page. After you select Handouts in the Format box of the Print File dialog box, click on **2**, **4**, or **6** to tell Freelance Graphics how many presentation pages you want on each printed page (see Figure 17.2). If your presentation pages include headers or footers, the header or footer will be printed on each page of the handout—not on each miniature presentation page.

Outlines   Make sure your presentation is displayed in Outline view before attempting to print the outline. Freelance Graphics prints all text that is currently showing in the outline (collapsed text does not print).

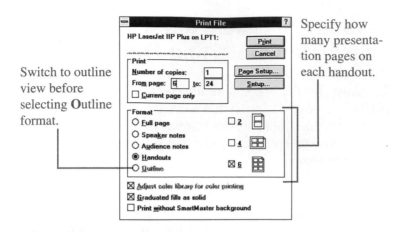

Switch to outline view before selecting **O**utline format.

Specify how many presentation pages on each handout.

Figure 17.2 Specify how many presentation pages you want on each handout page.

In this lesson, you learned how to print presentations, speaker notes, audience notes, handouts, and outlines. In the next lesson, you will learn how to add a symbol to your presentation.

Lesson 18

Adding
Symbols to Your
Presentation

In this lesson, you will learn how to add symbols to
your presentation, and how to edit those symbols.

Adding a Symbol to Your Presentation

Freelance Graphics symbols help make yourpresentation
more effective. Two of the page layouts, Title and Bullets
& Symbol, already contain Click here . . . symbol blocks
which you can use to add symbols. Additionally, you can
add a symbol to a page that doesn't contain any symbol
blocks.

Using Symbol Blocks

Freelance Graphics provides many symbols, arranged by
category. While most categories contain around six or
seven symbols, some categories hold only one symbol, and
others hold as many as twenty-four. You can browse
through the different symbols directly on your screen. To
add a symbol to a page containing a Click here . . . symbol
block, perform the following steps:

1. Select the Click here to add symbol prompt text. The Add Symbol to Page dialog box appears, as shown in Figure 18.1.

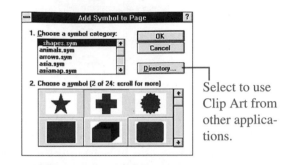

Figure 18.1   The Add Symbol to Page dialog box.

2. Select a symbol category from the list box. Freelance Graphics identifies how many symbols are available in that category and displays the symbol(s) at the bottom of the dialog box.

3. Scroll through the symbols box if the category you selected contains more than six symbols. Select the symbol you want to use.

4. Select OK. Freelance Graphics adds the symbol you selected to the Click here . . . symbol block, automatically sizing the symbol to fit into the block (see Figure 18.2).

Rearranging Symbols   Once you've added a symbol to your page, you can copy, move, or size the symbol just as you would any object. For details, read Lesson 20, "Managing Objects."

Symbol added to symbol blocks

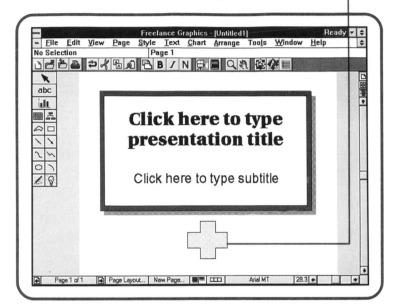

Figure 18.2 Freelance Graphics inserts the symbol into the symbol block.

Using the Add Symbol Icon

To add a symbol to a presentation page without a Click here . . . symbol block, perform the following steps:

1. Click the Add Symbol to Page icon located at the bottom right corner of the Toolbox (the light bulb icon). The Add Symbol to Page dialog box appears (see Figure 18.1).

2. Select the category you want.

3. Click on the symbol you want.

4. Select OK. Freelance Graphics adds the symbol to the page in its original size. To modify the size or position of the symbol, follow the procedures in Lesson 20, "Managing Objects."

My Chart Block Is Gone If you want to add a symbol to a page layout containing a chart, you should create the chart before making the symbol block. Otherwise, the symbol will be placed in the chart block after you use the Add a Symbol icon.

Editing a Symbol

To change the attributes of a symbol, perform the following procedures:

1. Double-click on the symbol. The Style Attributes dialog box appears, as shown in Figure 18.3.

2. Change the color, width, or style of the edge of the symbol (see Figure 18.4).

3. Change the color or pattern of the background area of the symbol (see Figure 18.4).

4. If you want to add a shadow to the symbol, select the Shadow scroll button to display a drop-down list of shadow types. Specify where you would like the drop shadow to be placed; Bottom Right was used for the symbol in Figure 18.4.

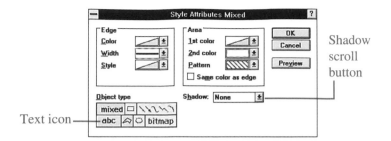

Figure 18.3 Change a symbol's attributes using the Style Attributes dialog box.

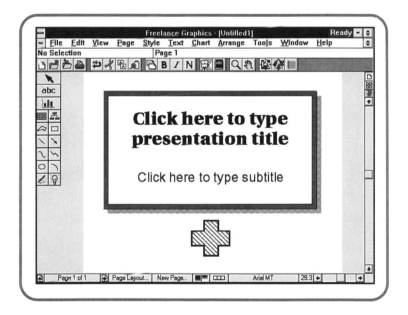

Figure 18.4 Changing the look of a symbol.

5. If the symbol contains text and you want to change the attributes of that text, click on the Text icon (the abc icon in the **O**bject Type area) underneath **O**bject Type.

107

This displays the Paragraph Styles dialog box. Modify the text attributes in this dialog box, and select OK.

6. To see a sample of what the symbol looks like with the changes, hold down the mouse button on the Preview button. Release the button and reconfigure the settings, if necessary.

7. Select OK. Freelance Graphics applies the new attributes to the symbol. Compare Figure 18.2 with Figure 18.4 to see how you can change the look of a symbol.

In this lesson, you learned how to add a symbol to your presentation and how to edit that symbol. In the next lesson, you will learn how to draw your own graphic objects.

Lesson 19
Drawing Objects

In this lesson, you will learn how to draw your own
objects using Toolbox instruments.

About Freelance Graphics Objects

In addition to supplying many symbols, Freelance Graphics lets you draw your own objects to suit your needs. Figure 19.1 shows you samples of drawings you can make.

The Toolbox, located at the left of your screen, provides all the instruments you'll need to create quality images. For a description of a tool's function, click the right mouse button on that tool and read the line at the top of the window. Or you can refer to the inside back cover of this book for a summary of Toolbox icon functions.

Toolbox   Polygon Ellipse   Rectangle   Arrow Square

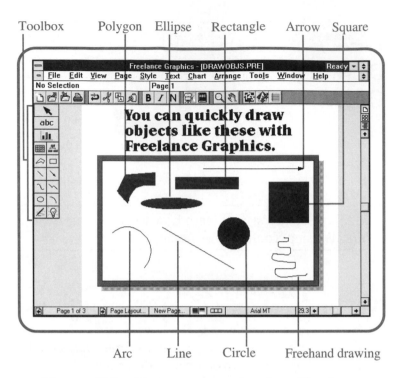

Arc   Line   Circle   Freehand drawing

Figure 19.1 You can create drawings like these using Toolbox instruments.

Making Your Drawings Precise

To help you draw with greater precision, Freelance Graphics can display a grid, rulers, and coordinate values. To draw measured objects, do one or more of the following:

Display a Grid To display a grid on the page to help you position and align objects, open the View menu, and select Units & Grids. The Units & Grids dialog box appears. Set the options you want, and then select OK. A grid appears on the page.

Display Rulers To display a horizontal or vertical ruler to help you measure objects as you draw, open the View menu, and select View Preferences. The View Preferences dialog box appears, as shown in Figure 19.2. Mark the Drawing ruler check box, and select OK. Rulers appear on the page.

Display Coordinate Values To display coordinates on the edit line as you work with objects, open the View menu, and select View Preferences. The View Preferences dialog box appears (see Figure 19.2). Mark the Coordinates check box, and select OK. Coordinate values are displayed on the edit line.

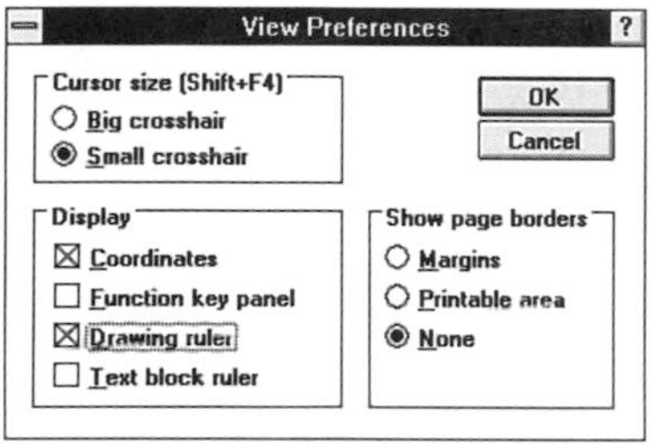

Figure 19.2 The View Preferences dialog box.

Drawing Objects

To begin the drawing process, follow these steps. Then refer to subsequent sections for details on how to create a particular type of object.

1. Select the icon in the Toolbox that represents the type of figure you want to draw. The mouse pointer changes to a crosshair, letting you know you can begin drawing.

111

2. Position the crosshair pointer where you want your figure to begin.

Enlarging the Crosshair If you prefer, you can make the crosshair larger. Open the View menu and select View Preferences. Mark Big crosshair in the View Preferences dialog box (see Figure 19.2).

It Takes Too Long Freelance Graphics redraws portions of the screen each time you edit an object. If you are drawing complex images, it may take a considerable amount of time for the redraw process to complete. To stop the redrawing process, press Esc. Later, when you're ready to have Freelance Graphics redraw the objects, press F9.

Lines and Arrows

To draw a line or arrow, complete these steps:

1. Click on the Line or Arrow icon from the Toolbox.

2. Drag the mouse the distance of the line or arrow. A dotted line appears as you draw, as shown in Figure 19.3. Press Shift as you drag the mouse to hold the line to 45 degree increments.

3. Release the mouse button to finish the line or arrow.

Select this icon to draw a line.

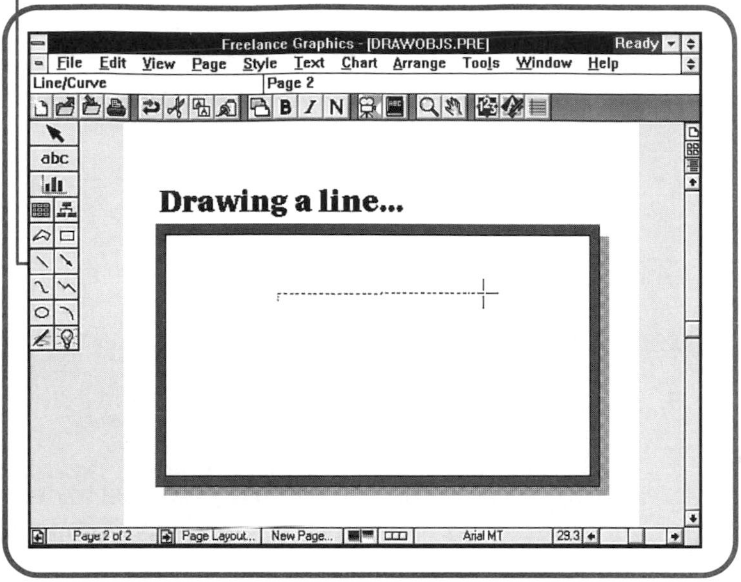

Figure 19.3 Drawing a line.

Altering the Arrowhead You can change the size of an arrowhead. Double-click on the arrow to display the Style Attributes Line & Curve dialog box. In the Arrowheads group box, select the desired size in the Size drop-down list.

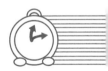

Polylines and Polygons

Use the Polyline icon to draw a segmented line. The polygon tool connects segmented lines to create a shape. Follow the steps below to draw a segmented line or a polygon:

113

1. Select the Polyline or Polygon icon from the Toolbox.

2. Drag the mouse the distance of the first segment. Freelance Graphics draws a dotted line (see Figure 19.3).

3. To start the next segment, as you continue to hold down the mouse button, press the Spacebar.

4. Drag the mouse to draw the length of the new segment.

5. Repeat steps 3 and 4 as needed.

6. Press Enter to finish the line or shape.

 **Completing a Polygon**   You do not need to draw the last side of the polygon; Freelance Graphics draws a line between the first and last line segments for you after you press Enter.

Rectangles, Squares, Circles, and Ellipses

To draw a rectangle, square, circle, or ellipse, complete these steps:

1. Select the tool you want to use from the toolbar.

2. Drag the mouse to size the rectangle, square, circle, or ellipse. An outline of the object appears. To make a square or a circle, press Shift as you drag.

3. Release the mouse button to complete the rectangle, square, circle, or ellipse.

Drawing Arcs

Follow these steps to draw an arc:

1. Select the Arc icon from the Toolbox.

2. Drag the mouse to make the correct length of the line, and then release the mouse button. Freelance Graphics draws a dotted line (see Figure 19.3).

3. Click on the line and drag the mouse to make the correct arc shape. Freelance Graphics draws a dashed outline of the arc as you draw, as shown in Figure 19.4.

4. Release the mouse button to finish the arc.

Select this icon to draw an arc.   Pull the line down from the arc.

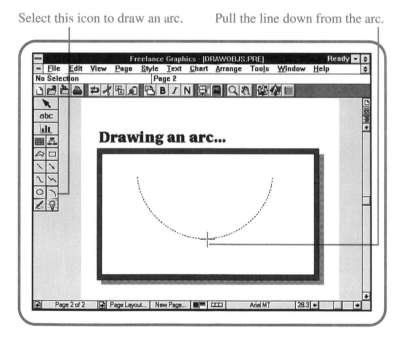

Figure 19.4   Drawing an arc.

Freehand Objects

Follow these steps to create a freehand drawing:

1. Select the Freehand Drawing icon from the Toolbox.

2. Drag the mouse in the shape of the image you want. As you drag, Freelance Graphics draws a line following the path you make.

3. If you want to move to a new location without drawing a line, press Backspace to temporarily stop drawing, and move the pointer to its new location.

In this lesson, you learned how to draw Freelance Graphics objects. In the next lesson, you will learn how to change the look of your objects.

Lesson 20
Managing Objects

In this lesson, you will learn how to select, move, size, and change the look of objects.

Selecting Objects

Before you can move or size an object, you must select it. To select one or more objects, do one of the following:

- To select one object, click on that object. Selection handles appear on the frame containing the object (see Figure 20.1). Clicking on one object deselects all other objects.

- To select multiple objects, click on the first object. Then press Shift as you click on each additional object. Selection handles appear on all selected objects, as seen in Figure 20.1.

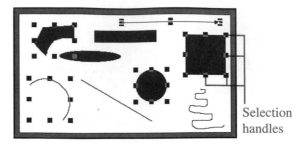

Selection handles

Figure 20.1   Selecting Multiple Objects.

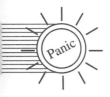

I Can't Select This Object   If you click on an object and it doesn't become selected, this means the object is part of the page layout and cannot be selected by clicking on it. You must open the Edit menu, select Edit Page Layouts, and then edit the object on the respective page layout.

Moving and Sizing Objects

To move or size an object, perform the following steps:

- To move an object, click on the object, and then drag it to a new location. Do not place the mouse pointer over a selection handle as you attempt to drag the object, otherwise the object's size rather than its location will change. Release the mouse button when you've reached the desired location.

- To size an object, position the mouse pointer over a selection handle until a two-headed arrow shows. Hold down the mouse button, and move the arrow in the appropriate direction to narrow, widen, shrink, or enlarge the size of the object. Release the mouse button when you've achieved the desired size.

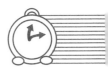

Moving or Copying an Object to Another Page To move or copy an object to another page, select the object, open the Edit menu, and select Cut to remove the object from the current page or Copy to leave a copy of the object on the current page. Display the page you want to move the object to, open the Edit menu, and select Paste.

Flipping an Object

You can change how an object looks by flipping. To flip an object from left to right or from top to bottom, perform the following steps:

1. Select the object you want to flip.

2. Open the Arrange menu, and select Flip.

3. Select Left to Right or Top to Bottom.

4. Freelance Graphics flips the object as specified. Figure 20.2 shows an object that has been flipped from top to bottom.

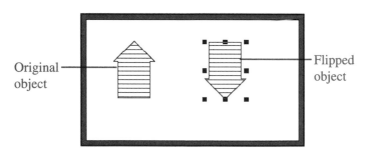

Figure 20.2   Flipping an object from top to bottom.

Rotating an Object

Freelance Graphics lets you rotate most objects. However, bitmaps can only be rotated in 90-degree increments, and tables, data charts, and organization charts cannot be rotated at all. To rotate an object, perform the following steps:

1. Select the object you want to rotate.

2. Open the Arrange menu, and select Rotate. The rotation pointer appears (see Figure 20.3).

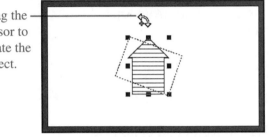

Drag the cursor to rotate the object.

Figure 20.3   Rotating an object.

3. Hold down the mouse button as you drag the mouse to rotate the object. A dotted outline displays the potential placement of the object.

Rotation Tricks   To achieve finer degrees of rotation, move the mouse further from the object as you drag. To hold the rotation movements to 45-degree increments, press Shift as you move the mouse.

4. When the temporary outline rests where you would like to position the object, release the mouse button. Freelance Graphics changes the object to its new configuration.

In this lesson, you learned how to select, move, size, and change the look of objects. In the next lesson, you will learn how to change the overall look of your presentation.

Lesson 21
Changing the Look of Your Presentation

In this lesson, you will learn how to modify the look of your presentation by using different SmartMaster sets and page layouts, and by switching from color to black and white.

Switching SmartMaster Sets

You can switch to a new SmartMaster set after you have created a presentation without loosing any presentation text because all SmartMaster sets contain the same eleven page layouts. The text you entered in the first SmartMaster set remains the same, but the text's format and placement change according to the specifications of the new SmartMaster set.

To switch to a new SmartMaster set, perform the following steps:

1. With any presentation page showing, open the Style menu, and select Choose SmartMaster Set. The Choose SmartMaster Set dialog box appears, as shown in Figure 21.1.

Figure 21.1 Select the new SmartMaster set in this dialog box.

2. Select the SmartMaster set you want. Review the sample illustration at the bottom of the dialog box after you select each SmartMaster set.

3. If you want to use a SmartMaster set without any graphics, mark the SmartMaster with blank background check box. This doesn't mean a generic SmartMaster set will be used. Rather, the placement and attributes of text will still follow the specifications of the SmartMaster set you chose, but graphics will not be included.

4. Select OK. Freelance Graphics applies the new SmartMaster set to your presentation.

Avoid Losing Your Edits It is important that you choose a SmartMaster set *before* you move or size objects. When you choose a new SmartMaster set, all changes made to the structure of your presentation pages will be lost.

123

Switching Page Layouts

Perhaps after creating a bulleted list you decide to place a chart next to the list, or you may want to include four rather than two charts on a presentation page. In either case, you don't have to start over from scratch, add new text or chart blocks, or do any moving or copying. Instead, just switch to a new page layout.

To assign a different page layout to a page, perform the following steps:

1. Display (or select in Page Sorter view) the page whose layout you want to change.

2. Open the Page menu, and select Choose Page Layout. The Choose Page Layout dialog box appears (see Figure 21.2).

3. Select the new page layout.

4. Select OK. Freelance Graphics rearranges the page structure using the new page layout.

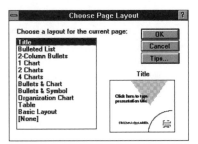

Figure 21.2 The Page Layout dialog box.

Switching to Black and White

If you do not have access to a color printer, you may want to see what your presentation looks like in black and white to get a better idea of how it will look printed. To switch from color to black and white, do one of the following:

- Open the Style menu, and select Use Black & White Palette. (To switch back to color, open the Style menu again, and select Use Color Palette.)

- Click on the Black & White icon in the box at the bottom of the window. (Click on the Color icon in the same box to switch back to color.)

- Press Alt+F9. This key works as a toggle between the color and black and white modes.

Printing in Black and White on a Color Printer To print in black and white on a color printer, you must switch to black and white mode before executing the print command. Otherwise, Freelance Graphics will print your presentation in color.

In this lesson, you learned how to change the overall look of your presentation by using new SmartMaster sets and page layouts, and by switching to black and white. In the next lesson, you will learn how to add finishing touches to your presentation.

Lesson 22

Adding Finishing Touches to Your Presentation

This lesson shows you how to add headers, footers, pictures, text, the current date, and the page number to every page in your presentation.

Using Headers and Footers

You can add headers and footers (which can include the current date and page number) to your printed presentation pages, keeping these points in mind:

- Headers and footers only appear on printed pages; they do not appear on your screen.

- The header and footer font is 10-point Arial or Arial MT. You cannot change the font or point size.

- Freelance Graphics positions headers and footers in the printable area of your page, not in the margins.

- Headers and footers can have up to 512 characters each.

• Each header and footer can have three parts: one left-aligned, one centered, and one right-aligned. Use the vertical bar character (|) to separate the parts of the header or footer (see the example in Figure 22.1). If you use only one header or footer, it will be left-aligned. If you want to center it, type a vertical bar before it. To right-align the header or footer, type two vertical bars in front of it.

Follow these procedures to add headers and footers to your printed presentation pages:

1. Open the File menu, and select Page Setup. The File Page Setup dialog box appears, as shown in Figure 22.1.

Figure 22.1 The File Page Setup dialog box.

2. Enter a header in the **H**eader box and/or footer in the **F**ooter box following the guidelines in Table 22.1.

3. Select OK. Though you don't see the headers or footers on your screen, they will be printed.

Table 22.1 Guidelines for printing headers and footers.

To print:	Do this:
The current date	Type the at character (@) where you want the date to be printed.
A header or footer of more than one line	Type a tilde (~) to start a new line.
Hidden characters (I, \, ~, #, @)	Type a backslash (\) before the hidden character if you want the hidden character to print.
Sequential page numbers	Type the number sign (#) where you want the page number to be printed.

Alternate Page Numbering Perhaps you want to print page numbers but don't want to start with Page 1. If so, type two number signs and then the starting page number. For example, you would type **##6** to print sequential page numbers starting with Page 6.

Adding Graphics or Text to Every Page

Imagine you want to include your company logo on each page of a lengthy presentation. It would be cumbersome to add a symbol block to each page to display the logo. Fortunately, with Freelance Graphics, you don't have to do this. Instead, you can place the symbol on the basic page layout of the SmartMaster set used for the presentation. The changes made to the basic page layout are reflected on every page of your presentation except the title page.

Permanent Changes? The changes you make to a SmartMaster set in the Edit Page Layout mode apply only to the currently opened presentation. They do not change the SmartMaster set itself or affect other presentations using that SmartMaster set.

To edit a SmartMaster page layout, perform the following steps:

1. Open the Edit menu, and select Edit Page Layouts, or press Shift+F9. The page layout used for the current page is displayed. Freelance Graphics changes the look of the area around the page so that you know you are editing a SmartMaster page layout rather than the page itself (text and graphics on your page do not show). Click on the Explain button located underneath the Toolbox if you need help on editing the page layout.

2. Select the Layout box at the bottom of the window to display the menu shown in Figure 22.2.

```
1.  Title
2.  Bulleted List
3.  2-Column Bullets
4.  1 Chart
5.  2 Charts
6.  4 Charts
7.  Bullets & Chart
8.  Bullets & Symbol
9.  Organization Chart
10. Table
✓11. Basic Layout
```

Figure 22.2   Editing a SmartMaster page layout.

3. Select number 11, Basic Layout. The page layout switches to Basic Layout.

4. Edit the page layout. Add symbols following the procedures in Lesson 18, "Adding a Symbol to Your Presentation," or text following the instructions in Lesson 5,
   "Entering and Editing Text." The symbols or text you
   add is placed on each presentation page, except the Title
   page (see Figure 22.3).

5. Click on the Page Sorter icon if you want to view the
   edited SmartMaster set (see Figure 22.3).

Page Sorter icon

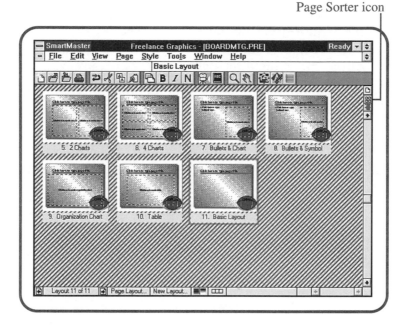

Figure 22.3 Viewing the edited SmartMaster set in
Page Sorter view.

6. To leave the edit mode and return to your presentation,
   click on the Return button located underneath the
   Toolbox, open the Edit menu, and select Edit Presentation Pages, or press Shift+F9.

In this lesson, you learned how to add headers, footers, graphics, and text to every presentation page. Congratulations on completing the *10 Minute Guide to Freelance Graphics for Windows*. In time, you're sure to grow in your knowledge and appreciation of Freelance Graphics for Windows.

Microsoft Windows Primer

Microsoft Windows is an interface program that makes your computer easier to use by allowing you to select menu items and pictures rather than type commands. Before you can take advantage of it, however, you must learn some Windows basics.

Starting Microsoft Windows

To start Windows, do the following:

1. At the DOS prompt, type **win**.

2. Press Enter.

The Windows title screen appears for a few moments, and then you see a screen like the one in Figure A.1.

What If It Didn't Work? You may have to change to the windows directory before starting Windows; to do so, type **CD \WINDOWS** and press Enter.

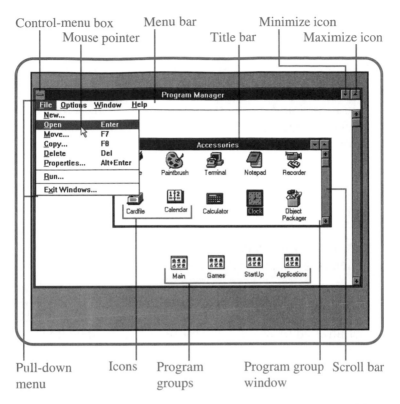

Control-menu box Menu bar Minimize icon
  Mouse pointer Title bar Maximize icon

Pull-down Icons Program Program group Scroll bar
menu   groups   window

Figure A.1 The Windows Program Manager with the File menu open.

Parts of a Windows Screen

As shown in Figure A.1, the Windows screen contains several unique elements that you won't see in DOS. Here's a brief summary.

Title bar. Shows the name of the window or program.

Program group windows. Contain program icons which allow you to run programs.

133

Icons. Graphic representations of programs. To run a program, you select its icon.

Minimize and Maximize buttons. Alter a window's size. The Minimize button shrinks the window to the size of an icon. The Maximize button expands the window to fill the screen. When maximized, a window contains a double-arrow *Restore* button, which returns the window to its original size.

Control-menu box. When selected, pulls down a menu that offers size and location controls for the window.

Pull-down menu bar. Contains a list of the pull-down menus available in the program.

Mouse Pointer. If you are using a mouse, the mouse pointer (usually an arrow) appears on-screen. It can be controlled by moving the mouse (discussed later in this primer).

Scroll bars. If a window contains more information than can be displayed in the window, a scroll bar appears. *Scroll arrows* on each end of the scroll bar allow you to scroll slowly. The *scroll box* allows you to scroll more quickly.

Using a Mouse

To work most efficiently in Windows, you should use a mouse. You can press mouse buttons and move the mouse in various ways to change the way it acts:

Point. Move the mouse pointer onto the specified item by moving the mouse. The tip of the mouse pointer must be touching the item.

Click on an item. Move the pointer onto the specified item, and press the mouse button once. Unless specified otherwise, use the left mouse button.

Double-click on an item. Move the pointer onto the specified item, and press and release the mouse button twice quickly.

Drag. Move the mouse pointer onto the specified item, hold down the mouse button, and move the mouse while holding down the button.

Figure A.2 shows how to use the mouse to perform common Windows activities, including running applications and moving and resizing windows.

Starting a Program

To start a program, simply select its icon. If the icon is contained in a program group window that's not open at the moment, open the window first. Follow these steps:

1. If necessary, open the program group window that contains the program you want to run. To open a program group window, double-click on its icon or press Ctrl+Tab to select the icon, and press Enter.

2. Double-click on the icon for the program you want to run or use the arrow keys to select the icon, and press Enter.

Click to control   Drag title bar   Click to
window size   to move   Click to shrink. expand.
and location.   window.

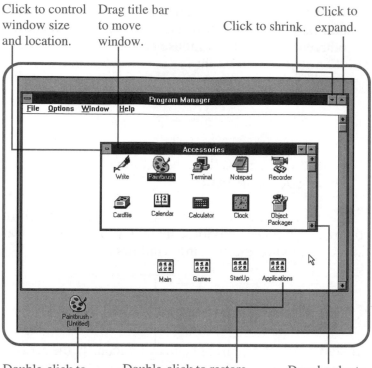

Double-click to   Double-click to restore   Drag border to
restore application.   the program group window.   size window.

Figure A.2   Use your mouse to control Windows.

Using Menus

The pull-down menu bar (see Figure A.3) contains various menus from which you can select commands. Each Windows program that you run has a set of pull-down menus; Windows itself has a set, too.

To open a menu, select its name on the menu bar. Once a menu is open, you can select a command from it by clicking on the desired command or pressing the underlined letter. Or you can highlight the command with the arrow keys and press Enter.

Shortcut Keys Notice that in Figure A.3, some commands are followed by key names, such as Enter (for the **O**pen command) or F8 (for the **C**opy command). These are called *accelerator keys*. You can use these keys to perform these commands without even opening the menu.

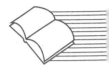

Dimmed options   Shortcut keys

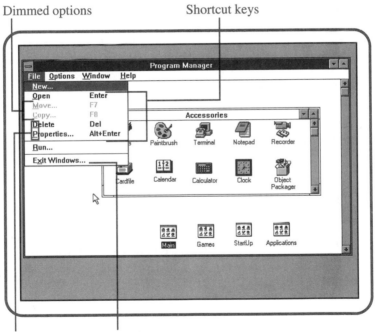

Selection letters   Ellipsis

Figure A.3 A menu lists various commands you can perform.

Usually, when you select a command, the command is performed immediately. However

- If the command name is gray (rather than black), the command is unavailable at the moment, and you cannot choose it.

- If the command name is followed by an arrow, selecting the command will cause another menu to appear, from which you select another command.

- If the command name is followed by an ellipsis (three dots), selecting it will cause a dialog box to appear. You'll learn about dialog boxes in the next section.

Navigating Dialog Boxes

A dialog box is Windows' way of requesting additional information. For example, if you choose Print from the File menu, you'll see the dialog box shown in Figure A.4.

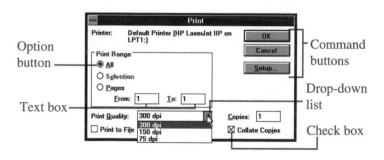

Figure A.4 A typical dialog box.

Each dialog box contains one or more of the following elements:

- *List boxes* display available choices. To activate a list, click inside the list box. If the entire list is not visible, use the scroll bar to view the items in the list. To select an item from the list, click on it.

- *Drop-down lists* are similar to list boxes, but only one item in the list is shown. To see the rest of the items, click on the down arrow to the right of the list box. To select an item from the list, click on it.

- *Text boxes* allow you to type an entry. To activate a text box, click inside it. To edit an existing entry, use the arrow keys to move the cursor, and the Del or Backspace keys to delete existing characters, and then type your correction.

- *Check boxes* allow you to select one or more items in a group of options. For example, if you are styling text, you may select Bold and Italic to have the text appear in both bold and italic type. Click on a check box to activate it.

- *Option buttons* are like check boxes, but you can select only one option button in a group. Selecting one button unselects any option that is already selected. Click on an option button to activate it.

- *Command buttons* execute (or cancel) the command once you have made your selections in the dialog box. To press a command button, click on it.

Switching Between Windows

Many times, you will have more than one window open at once. Some open windows may be program group windows, while others may be actual programs that are running. To switch among them, you can:

- Pull down the Window menu and choose the window you want to view.

  OR

- If a portion of the desired window is visible, click on it.

Controlling a Window

As you saw earlier, you can minimize, maximize, and restore windows on your screen. But you can also move them and change their size.

- To move a window, drag its title bar to a different location. (Remember, *drag* means to hold down the left mouse button while you move the mouse.)

- To resize a window, position the mouse pointer on the border of the window until you see a double-headed arrow; then drag the window border to the desired size.

Copying Your Program Disks with File Manager

Before you install any new software, you should make a copy of the original disks as a safety precaution. Windows' File Manager makes this process easy.

First, start File Manager by double-clicking on the File Manager icon in the Main program group. Then, for each disk you need to copy, follow these steps:

1. Locate a blank disk of the same type as the original disk, and label it to match the original. Make sure the disk you select does not contain any data that you want to keep.

2. Place the original disk in your disk drive (A or B).

3. Open the Disk menu, and select Copy Disk. The Copy Disk dialog box appears.

4. Select the drive used in step 2 from the Source In list box.

5. Select the same drive from the Destination In list box. (Don't worry; File Manager will tell you to switch disks at the appropriate time.)

6. Select OK. The Confirm Copy Disk dialog box appears.

7. Select Yes to continue.

8. When instructed to insert the Source disk, choose OK, since you already did this at step 2. The Copying Disk box appears, and the copy process begins.

9. When instructed to insert the target disk, remove the original disk from the drive and insert the blank disk. Then choose OK to continue. The Copying Disk box disappears when the process is complete.

Index